PREPPER'S
FINANCIAL GUIDE

DISCARD

PREPPER'S FINANCIAL GUIDE

STRATEGIES *to* INVEST, STOCKPILE *and* BUILD SECURITY *for* TODAY *and* THE POST-COLLAPSE MARKETPLACE

JIM COBB

Ulysses Press

Published in the U.S. by
Ulysses Press
P.O. Box 3440
Berkeley, CA 94703
www.ulyssespress.com

ISBN: 978-1-61243-403-2
Library of Congress Control Number 2014943039

Printed in Canada by Marquis Book Printing

10 9 8 7 6 5 4 3 2 1

Acquisitions Editor: Keith Riegert
Managing Editor: Claire Chun
Editor: Renee Rutledge
Proofreader: Lauren Harrison
Indexer: Sayre Van Young
Cover design: Noah Mercer
Interior design: Jake Flaherty
Cover photos: stock market © JMiks/shutterstock.com; money © Bjorn Hoglund/shutterstock.com; garden © Hannamariah/shutterstock.com; gold © Pics-xl/shutterstock.com; solar panels © Elena Elisseeva/shutterstock.com; jars © Elena Elisseeva/shutterstock.com; safe © Pinosub/shutterstock.com

Distributed by Publishers Group West

NOTE TO READERS: This book is independently authored and published and no sponsorship or endorsement of this book by, and no affiliation with, any trademarked product mentioned or pictured within is claimed or suggested. All trademarks that appear in the text in this book belong to their respective owners and are used here for informational purposes only. The author and publisher encourage readers to patronize the recommended products mentioned in this book. This book has been written and published strictly for informational purposes, and in no way should be used as a substitute for actual instruction with qualified professionals. The author and publisher are providing you with information in this work so that you can have the knowledge and can choose, at your own risk, to act on that knowledge. The author and publisher also urge all readers to be aware of their health status, to consult local fish and game laws, and to consult health care and outdoor professionals before engaging in any potentially hazardous activity. Any use of the information in this book is made on the reader's good judgment. The author and publisher assume no liability for personal injury to the reader or others harmed by the reader, property damage, consequential damage or loss, however caused, from using the information in this book.

For Bob and Joanne Hrodey—I could never thank you both enough for your support, guidance, and friendship.

CONTENTS

ACKNOWLEDGMENTS

If you've read any of my other books, you'll no doubt recognize at least a few of these usual suspects.

As always, I must thank my beautiful wife and my awesome boys. I simply could not ask for a more supportive and understanding family. They have often gone without my presence as I work on books or travel out of town for appearances and speaking engagements. I love you all dearly. I will readily admit that my wife, Tammy, has taught me more about financial planning than anyone else. Without her guidance, I'd have probably ended up living in a very small apartment with the words THIS END UP printed on the walls.

To my dad, thanks for always encouraging me and asking about my writing. Your support means a lot to me. Love you, Pop!

Big thanks to David Vlosak, George Williams College of Aurora University for his input on some of the historical elements in Chapter 1. Any errors are mine, not his.

To John McCann, thank you for not only contributing the Foreword for this book but for your friendship and support. When we do finally get together at an expo or something, the first round is on me.

Huge thanks to Keith Riegert and the rest of the team at Ulysses Press. As always, working with you folks is just a dream.

To all of you members of the Professional Prepared Bloggers Association, thank you so much for your support, as well as all the tips and tricks you've shown me. I hope I'm able to return the favor someday.

To Sharon Ahern, please know that you and Jerry (may he rest in peace) are directly responsible for my chosen career path today. Your books were, and still are, a constant source of inspiration.

Finally, once again I must thank my amigo Chris Golden for his constant support and frequent advice. My friend, there is no way I'd have gotten this far without you.

FOREWORD

First of all, I commend Jim Cobb on writing a book that fills a void in the plethora of other books that have been written in the prepper and preparedness genre. *Prepper's Financial Guide* provides the reader with an entire dissertation on a subject that usually gets little, if any, coverage in books meant to provide you with information about preparing for a disaster. What could be more disastrous than the loss of your savings, or the devaluation of the currency that you depend on to purchase your needs?

Take heed of the information provided here. It is essential that you pay attention and learn the lessons that will help you prepare for a situation that could occur at a moment's notice. I have long been an advocate of studying financial history as a means to protect myself from mistakes made in the past. The history of previous economic collapses is presented here, illustrating that they have happened before and most likely will again. When banks close and your ATM doesn't work, what is your strategy for survival?

Many people today seem to want to follow the example of our government. If deficit spending is good for them, then it is good for you. It is, as our current deficit reflects, a recipe for disaster, both for our government and those who spend more than they make. Jim spends considerable time on presenting an approach for debt reduction, which is an important first step. He then describes the steps necessary to create a budget to ensure that you don't spend more than you make. The results will provide you with those additional finances for preparedness.

Currency is only worth something if people believe it is so. Currencies today are backed by nothing more than public support of their worth. Jim provides important information on commodity currency and fiat currency. I have always been a big advocate of owning some foreign currency in the event that US currency fails. Jim takes time to address the currencies of other nations in order to provide you with options other than the currency of your own country.

As you will learn, currencies are fallible, but gold and silver will always be worth something. Jim discusses important information about precious metals, as well as minerals, to help you select those that will assist you in protecting your wealth.

A chapter I really like, "Bartering Skills Instead of Stuff," addresses a central aspect of preparedness. I have discussed this in books and articles, and Jim does it justice. When money fails to be useful, the skills you have available will provide you with a means to obtain what you need without money.

Of course, once you have valuable assets, you will need to protect them. If banks fail to open and you can't get your hands on it, your money will be of little use. Jim provides various options for the protection of other valuables that will also need securing.

Of course, money and skills are not your only means with which to barter or obtain wealth. Gardening and the preservation of food is an asset. Producing your own honey and harvesting your own meat provide assets. This book presents many more types of activities that present potential options based on your location or skills.

The bottom line is that this book is important for anyone who is concerned with emergency preparedness or becoming more self-reliant. Buy it, read it, and adjust your strategy to ensure that your finances, and the ability to transact for those things you need in an emergency situation, are a part of your overall plan.

John D. McCann
SurvivalResources.com
Author of *Practical Self-Reliance* and
Bug-Out—Reality vs. Hype

CHAPTER 1

WHAT IS ECONOMIC COLLAPSE?

A *depression* involves a long-term downward swing in the economy. Unemployment goes up and available credit goes down. Businesses, and, occasionally, banks close up shop. Those who have money generally spend less of it, which turns the whole thing into sort of a vicious circle. With fewer people buying goods, manufacturers sell less. This reduces their income so they need to let employees go, which means more people with less money. An *economic collapse* is an economic depression cranked up to eleven, with a healthy sprinkling of loan defaults, devalued currency, and reduced trade with other countries.

Economic collapse is a bit different from other types of disasters preppers often discuss. In those scenarios, there is vast destruction and damage to infrastructure. In an economic collapse, there may very well be *some* damage as a result of civil unrest, but nothing on the scale of, say, a major earthquake along the New Madrid Fault. Along these same lines, other types of disasters often involve some sort of massive die-off, such as what we'd expect to see if the Yellowstone Caldera were to blow. An economic collapse wouldn't really have much of a direct impact in that way.

In other words, an economic collapse is a disaster without the death and destruction.

The other major difference is the speed, or lack thereof, with which an economic collapse hits. A chain of events lead up to a collapse, and these steps happen over a lengthy period of time. It isn't like everything is fine when you go to bed one night, then in the morning, the dollar suddenly isn't worth squat, nobody has a job, and the bank is taking your home from you. A collapse is very much akin to that old proverb about the frog in a pot of water on the stove, slowly coming to a boil.

The threat of economic collapse is nothing new. In numerous instances in history, one country or another has endured financial strife. Let's take a short walk through the last hundred years or so and talk about a few of the major ones.

GERMANY (1921–1924)

After the conclusion of World War I, the world in general was a bit miffed with Germany for having instigated the whole mess, as they saw it at least. France, Belgium, and many other European countries had been devastated by the war. By signing the Treaty of Versailles on June 28, 1919, Germany, under protest, took all of the blame and faced severe sanctions. In addition to giving up land and reducing the German army drastically, the country also had to pay reparations. The idea was that Germany had to pay, either in cash or with material goods, for the damage other countries had suffered. Now, you know how you've always been told not to sign a contract without reading it?

Well, the Treaty of Versailles didn't specify an exact figure for those reparations. But Germany really didn't have much choice; it was either sign the Treaty or be invaded by the Allies. Not to mention, the Allies had the country locked up fairly well due to naval blockades, and many citizens were starving.

The first installment payment of about 2 billion gold marks was paid in 1921. Most of this payment consisted not of cash but material goods such as coal and wood. Nonetheless, the amount of hard currency that was paid depleted Germany's finances greatly. They began to purchase foreign currency, which flooded the market with German marks. This resulted in a devaluation of the mark, meaning it took even more marks to make these purchases.

The following year, Germany found it was unable to make the next installment payment. Not unlike a collection agency calling you about an old credit card balance, France in particular thought Germany was full of *merde*. France and Belgium invaded Germany's most valuable industrial area, the Ruhr. The German government responded by issuing an order telling all workers in that area to go on strike and passively resist the occupying forces.

As a result of those orders, Germany's economy suffered. The country wasn't producing any goods, so no money was coming in, but those striking workers were being paid to resist. Of course, it also costs money just to operate a government. On top of that, the French and Belgian forces dealt with resisting citizens by kicking them out of their homes, leaving the German government to take care of them.

Germany finally decided enough was enough and began printing more money, which was about the worst thing they could have chosen to do. Foreign investors saw this as evidence that the country was in a world of financial hurt, so they took their toys and went home. By printing more and more money, without anything backing the value, hyperinflation resulted. Inflation is when prices go up and the buying power of currency goes down. We deal with this every day, right? I mean, what did a gallon of gas cost when you started driving? Hyperinflation, however, takes this to a whole new level. Prices on common goods skyrocketed into the stratosphere in a very short period. A loaf of bread in Germany cost about 160 marks in 1922. By the next year, the price had gone up to 1,500,000 marks, then quickly rose to 200,000,000,000 marks in short order.

Can you imagine buying anything that costs billions of dollars? Remember, we're talking cash here. If you accepted a check, its value would have dropped by the time you took it to the bank. How did people carry that much cash with them? Wheelbarrows, mostly.

Helpful tip: If your government decides it needs to create ever-larger denominations of paper money, just to keep up with inflation, that's a clue something is amiss.

It got to the point where workers were paid every hour and family members rushed to spend the money as quickly as they could, as prices were rising constantly. As is often the case, the poor got poorer. Those who had scrimped and saved their entire lives suddenly found their hard-earned money worthless. The rich citizens typically owned land and they could produce their own food because of that. The middle class and below, however, didn't have that luxury. Many sold off family treasures and heirlooms just to survive. Furniture was broken up and tossed into the fireplace so the family could keep warm.

Finally, in September of 1923, a new chancellor, Gustav Stresemann, told workers in the Ruhr to get back to their jobs. The German mark was replaced with a new currency, one backed by American gold. The German reparation payments were reduced to a much more manageable size. Within a few years, the economy improved markedly. People were back to work and prices fell to normal levels again.

UNITED STATES (1929–1940)

Even today, experts disagree on what exactly caused the Great Depression. Many people, when they give it any thought at all, tend to believe the stock market crash of 1929 is synonymous with the Great Depression. However, the crash was merely one of several factors involved.

During World War I, American farmers were rather prosperous. Due to the war, their produce brought in a good income. Many of them borrowed from banks so as to increase their land as well as purchase better equipment, all in an attempt to produce even more crops. But, once the war was over, prices on farm crops fell and many of these same farmers found themselves struggling to make the loan payments. As a result, banks ended up losing money on those loans. Even though they could, and in many cases did, foreclose on those farms, they didn't recoup their losses.

Those defaulted loans, as well as the loans larger banks made to foreign countries that never repaid, resulted in many banks closing up. The banks that were able to stay in business became very reluctant to issue new loans. In something of a vicious cycle, as banks folded, a large number of customers simultaneously rushed to their own banks to withdraw all of their deposits. When such bank runs happen, the problem is that banks don't generally have as much cash on hand as their total deposits may indicate and consequently run out. This tends to make customers a bit panicky, which leads to more people showing up demanding their money—not typically a fun time for anyone involved.

During the 1920s, the stock market did extremely well and many people made quite a bit of money with trading. However, a lot of those stock purchases were *on margin*, meaning the purchaser only paid a portion of the actual price, with the balance paid when the stock was sold again. Not a bad system as long as everything is going well. I buy a hundred shares of XYZ Widgets Limited at $10 a share, but only actually pay half of that cost. Then, when I sell my shares to someone else for $30 a share, the other $500 I owed is taken from the profit. Simple and easy, right? When the market crashed in 1929, all of those people who had bought on margin now needed to come up with the money they owed for what were now worthless stocks. And, once again, banks took a hit too because many people had taken out loans to buy stock and after the crash lacked the funds to make their payments.

Oh, by the way, all those bank failures? This was before deposits were insured, so when the banks went belly up, all the money people had entrusted to the bank disappeared forever.

Due to all the bank closings and other economic woes, people began to buy less and less, trying to save what little they could. This lack of purchasing led to companies holding more and more inventory, with little to show for it. Layoffs became common. This meant many people couldn't afford to make the payments on the installment loans they'd take out when times were good. Yet again, banks took the hit.

In 1930, the federal government, in its infinite wisdom, created the Hawley-Smoot Tariff. The idea was to protect failing American manufactures and farmers by charging a high tax on imports to the United States. In doing so, it was hoped consumers would be more inclined to buy domestic goods, since the prices on imports would go up to offset the tariff. All well and good on the surface, but the result was many foreign companies decided not to do business with America altogether. Not only did this reduce the imports to the United States, but some of those other countries decided they didn't need our products either, reducing our exports as well.

OK, so far we have banks closing all over the place, taking all the cash with them, the stock market crash, and foreign investors reducing or outright ceasing to do business with the United States. What else could we add to this recipe for disaster?

Drought, that's what. Massive, interminable drought throughout America's Great Plains during the 1930s. While drought isn't something that can really be predicted, let alone combated, it is worth noting just how much mankind actually contributed to the repercussions.

The Dust Bowl encompassed the panhandles of Oklahoma and Texas, as well as portions of New Mexico, Colorado, and Kansas. Back in the mid- to late-1800s and into the 1900s, the United States government offered land in these areas to settlers. We're not talking a puny lot suitable for a suburban home, either. Think big—initially 160 acres per family and later expanded to 300-plus. Now, this area of the country wasn't known for being all that awesome for crops, what with the general lack of surface water. But, coincidentally, around the early 1900s, unusually wet weather settled in the region, causing settlers to believe the climate had changed for the better. Many of these homesteaders who arrived in droves began large-scale agricultural endeavors, taking full advantage of mechanized plows and combines.

As the prices for crops increased due to World War I, the amount of land in the area devoted to agriculture multiplied exponentially. Hey, there was money to be made, right? Well, that came at a cost. All that agriculture churned up the soil, eliminating the grasses that had been holding the dirt in place during dry spells. Guess what happened when that wet weather went away?

In 1930, drought settled over the region, affecting crops and drying out the soil. As anyone who has lived in or traveled through the area could tell you, the winds get quite powerful from time to time, what with not much of anything to impede them for miles on end.

So, what happens when you have extremely dry soil coupled with high winds? That's right, boys and girls, you get dust storms. In this case, we're talking dust storms of biblical proportions. Millions of pounds of topsoil were stripped from the land, carried aloft, and deposited as far away as Chicago and beyond. This was not a one-time event, either, but repeated over and over during the course of the next few years.

As a result of the massive crop failures, many families in the plains states gave up and moved on. In many cases, the dust storms themselves destroyed homes, leaving families little choice but to seek new lives elsewhere. Those who had financed their land through a bank lost the property through foreclosure. From 1930–1940, well over three million people pulled up stakes and headed west, hoping to find fortune or at least a better life.

During the early years of the Great Depression, families that still had an income saw it drop around 40 percent. Think about that. Could your family readily handle losing almost half of its income? Somewhere upward of 10,000 banks failed during that same time frame. What if your bank suddenly went belly up, taking your money with it?

While historians argue as much about what stopped the Great Depression as they do about what caused it, most agree that the entry of the United States into World War II marked the Depression's final end, at least for Americans.

It is worth noting that the Great Depression wasn't limited to the United States. It was felt at every corner of the planet, to one degree or another. Global trade overall declined and countries that relied heavily upon exports, such as Australia, were particularly hard hit.

ARGENTINA (1998-2002)

In the late 1990s, several factors came together and led to a severe economic collapse in Argentina. Back in 1991, the Argentinean *peso* was legally valued at a one-to-one basis to the dollar. Those so inclined could go to a bank and convert ten pesos to ten dollars without any sort of trouble. The problem came in 1999 when Brazil devalued its own currency, the *real*. Now, if ground beef cost you $3.99 per pound at one store, but only $1.49 per pound for the exact same thing at a store across the street, where would you shop? That's pretty much what many investors and foreign buyers did when confronted with the same decision—they started buying from Brazil instead of Argentina. As a result, Argentina saw their exports rapidly decline, which greatly reduced the money coming into the country.

Corruption played a key role as well. Government spending was quite high through the 1990s and debt was piling up. The International Monetary Fund continued to lend the country money, though Argentina had little to show in the way of ability to repay the loans. Money was being funneled into offshore accounts, rather than being invested back into the country. This caused interest rates to go up, which led to many businesses closing when they were unable to keep up with payments.

As more and more people lost their jobs, tax revenues declined. It is awfully difficult for someone with no money to pay taxes, right?

Then, in late 1999, Argentine President Fernando de la Rua began a series of austerity measures in an attempt to forestall a complete collapse. These included reducing government spending and instituting pay cuts to civil servants. These austerity measures went on through 2001, with little to no real improvement to the economy.

In November of 2001, citizens who still had money in their banks began to withdraw all or most of their balances, causing a bank run.

The government's reaction to these bank runs was to institute measures that basically froze all bank accounts for a year, allowing for only small withdrawals of cash. As you might expect, citizens were decidedly less than thrilled. They took to the streets of Buenos Aires and elsewhere, marching and banging pots and pans. These demonstrations soon took a turn toward violence and destruction.

On December 21, 2001, President De la Rua resigned and fled the country, along with most of his cabinet. Interim President Rodriguez Saa was quickly replaced with Eduardo Duhalde, but not before the Saa-run government defaulted on a large amount of public debt, roughly $130 billion.

One of the first things President Duhalde did was abandon the peso-to-dollar exchange rate that had been fixed at one-to-one for so long. The peso began to decline in value on the open market. The government also declared that all funds held in banks would be converted to pesos from dollars. This resulted in a significant loss for many people. Just how angry would you be if the $5,000 you had squirreled away in a savings account was suddenly worth only about $2,700?

Throughout these years, unemployment reached about 25 percent; in some neighborhoods, the number rose to half the population. With so many people out of work and with little to no money available for buying necessities, barter became very popular. In addition, citizens did everything they could to find food, including hunting or trapping cats and dogs. Rat casserole, anyone?

Thousands of people lost their homes and ended up living on the streets, finding shelter under bridges or in makeshift shanty towns. In the wake of so many business closures, workers at some of these companies took over the facilities, creating cooperatively owned enterprises. There were also numerous assemblies, akin to neighborhood meetings, where citizens worked together to provide solutions for obtaining food and medical care, among other necessities.

By 2003, the economy had somewhat stabilized. The devaluation of the peso actually had a positive impact on Argentinean exports, with goods now being cheaper than the competition's. This allowed for a massive influx of foreign currency into the country. In turn, Argentina was able to retire its debt to the International Monetary Fund several years ahead of schedule.

THE GREAT RECESSION (2007-2009)

The Great Recession, sometimes referred to as the Global Financial Crisis, occurred in 2007–2009 and its effects are still being felt at the time of this writing in late 2014. One of the primary factors that led to the Great Recession was the so-called "housing bubble." Beginning in the late 1990s and peaking in 2006, real estate values skyrocketed. At the same time, mortgage lenders, under pressure from their shareholders to keep increasing profits, became more and more lax about their lending practices. People who in years past would never have qualified for a mortgage were suddenly being told they could afford homes that vastly exceeded their normal budget. This was due to the use of an Adjustable Rate Mortgage (ARM), which essentially allowed the homebuyer to enjoy very reduced mortgage payments for the loan's first couple of years. The plan for many of these buyers was to "flip" the home before the ARM kicked in and their mortgage payments increased substantially.

For some people, this plan worked out very well and they ended up making a fair amount of money on the deal. Many, many others, though, abruptly found out what happens when your credit has been overextended. When those mortgage payment amounts went up, they weren't able to pay them. As they missed more and more payments, they tried selling their homes but there weren't any buyers who were willing and/or able to pay the inflated asking prices. Banks began foreclosing on the properties and were forced to try selling them at a loss. Again, though, they found few buyers as there were so many people in the same boat.

On top of that, it was later learned that some lenders were engaging in what came to be called "robo-signing." This was when mortgages and other loans were approved even though they didn't meet the actual loan guidelines. In some cases, the loan applications were missing information or necessary documentation, but were still approved.

Several banks were on the verge of closing because they had so much of their capital tied up in these failed real estate deals. The federal government finally had to step in and bail out these banks by purchasing some of the bad debt, which served to increase the available funds to the banks.

There were other causes as well that contributed to the whole mess, such as predatory lending and a lack of proper regulation. However, when you boil it all down and dispense with all the fancy terminology, it really just comes down to greed. Greedy shareholders, looking to line their silk pockets with more cash. Greedy banks, hoping to increase their investments. Greedy homeowners, buying houses any twelve-year-old could have said there's no way they could afford. It is all pretty sickening, when you stop to think about it. The haste to make as much money as quickly as possible nearly caused a complete collapse of the financial system.

As a result of the Great Recession, many lenders have made changes to how and to whom they lend money, whether for mortgages or other types of loans. Credit has become much more restricted, though it is still fairly easy to get a credit card, provided you meet minimal requirements. Even now, in 2015, many homeowners are facing foreclosure due to their inability to either make the payments or sell off the property.

What would have happened had the government not stepped in and bailed out the banks and other companies that were being affected by the recession? Most of them would have closed up shop, taking with them the funds that were owned by their customers. Millions of people across the country would have woken up one morning and found they didn't have a bank account anymore. While there are avenues they could have pursued to get those funds back, none of them work overnight. Pretty hard to buy groceries if all you have for currency is a letter from your bank, telling you they'll repay you...someday.

WHAT WOULD A UNITED STATES ECONOMIC COLLAPSE LOOK LIKE TODAY?

Imagine: The company you work for is one of the few in the area still operating, for now at least. Granted, your paycheck has been cut almost in half due to wage reductions, but something is better than nothing. On your way to work, you see gas has jumped in price again, almost $9 a gallon now. Luckily, you live close enough that you can ride your bike to work, which saves you gas, but isn't going to be much fun in a month or so when the snow starts flying.

Imagine: You go into a store to buy groceries and your credit card is refused. I don't mean, "Excuse me, Sir, your card has been...declined," I mean the store won't take any credit cards or even checks. As you dig into your wallet to see how much cash you have on hand, an announcement comes over the loudspeaker, informing everyone that the store will be closing in fifteen minutes, even though it is the middle of the day.

Imagine: Stopping at the ATM on your way home from work, the screen tells you the ATM is out of order. You then see a sign taped to the door of the bank. "Bank Holiday—Closed Until Further Notice." Some quick mental math, adding what is in your pocket to what you have stashed at home, concludes you have a whopping $52 to your name. With milk running around $8 a gallon and bread at $5 a loaf, this isn't good.

Our world is far different today than it was back in the 1930s. Our society today is one of immediate gratification. Whether we're talking about the latest hit single from Susie Cantsingbutlooksgreatinabikini or a half-caf, no foam, I'll-smash-this-bottle-and-cut-you-if-you-forget-the-sprinkles-again double latte, just about anything can be had with a simple click of a mouse or swipe of a credit card. The thought of actually saving up for something you want is lost on many people. As a result, should extreme hard times come again, like they did in the days of the Great Depression, many of these people will become exceedingly desperate.

Think about it like this. Ever gone shopping on Black Friday? If you have, or if you watch the inevitable news footage later, you know all too well just how crazy people can get over a cheap toaster or hot new toy. Now, imagine it isn't the latest Elmo doll they're after, but food.

Generally speaking, people in the United States were much more self-reliant back in the days of the Great Depression than they are today. Many city residents then still knew basic skills like scratch cooking. Today, not so much. Take a poll among your friends and ask them if they know how to darn a sock, dress a squirrel, or change the oil in their car. Unless you hang out with some pretty cool people who are already in tune with being self-sufficient, the answer to most or all of those is going to be a resounding no, possibly with laughter thrown in for good measure.

Those who aren't prepared to meet their own needs, who haven't taken steps to be more self-reliant, are going to get desperate in short order as their normal avenues for obtaining resources become unavailable. A savings account with a five-digit balance does you no good if you can't access the funds or if the funds are suddenly worthless. A credit card with a full $10,000 of available credit isn't going to be of much help if stores aren't accepting plastic. Even gold or silver coins, while beneficial, as we'll discuss later, aren't going to fill your belly or keep you warm.

In the wake of a full collapse, expect riots, looting, and other instances of civil unrest. For this reason, among others, you should avoid any large assemblies of people, particularly in an urban area. Keep your head down and stay out of the way of the crowd as best you can. Without trying to sound like an extremist, the thought of another civil war, this one between the "haves" and the "have-nots," really isn't out of the realm of possibility, should a crisis linger too long.

Suffice it to say, an economic collapse in the United States will be harsh, ugly, and just not a lot of fun for all involved.

CHAPTER **2**

DEBT REDUCTION

In today's society, it can be very difficult to get through life without incurring some manner of debt. Not impossible by any stretch, but difficult. Few people today set aside funds and save up for major purchases. Thus, they rely on bank loans of one sort or another. The problem comes in when you end up with so many credit bills that you find it nearly impossible to even make the minimum payments every month. Tack on the interest and it becomes extremely unlikely you'll ever get ahead, or so it seems.

Now, I'm not going to sit here and give you the "holier than thou" spiel. What I am going to do, though, is share with you some tips and tricks that may help you get out from underneath the debt umbrella. Maybe not completely but at least to the degree that you don't feel as though your world is crashing about your ears.

Before we get into that, though, let's talk a minute about why this sort of information is included in a book about disaster readiness. No matter how you approach the issue, prepping costs money. Those funds need to come from somewhere. If you are so cash-strapped you can hardly afford that double latte every day, you're probably going to find it difficult to invest much of anything into your preps. So, to put it simply, the more money you can save elsewhere in the budget, the more you can put toward prepping.

Plus, there is also a psychological component at work here. Debt causes stress, to put it mildly. The more you owe, the more stress you likely have in your life. All of the energy you expend in fighting that stress could certainly be put to better use.

CREATING A BUDGET

The first step in solving a problem is recognizing it, right? To that end, we need to figure out where the holes in our boat are so we can plug them and prevent future leaking. Many of us, even if we don't have a formal written budget, have at least a pretty good idea of where our money goes every month. We know, for example, our car payment is $225 each month, our rent or mortgage payment is a set amount, our auto insurance is due every six months. That's the easy stuff to calculate. For most people, though, it is the nickel and dime stuff that kills us each month.

Here's what I want you to do. Sit down and make a list of every bill you pay each month, everything from your rent/mortgage to credit card bills. Every account you need to pay on a monthly basis goes on this list. Don't worry about incidentals, we'll get to those in a bit.

Next, write down the bills you have each year but perhaps not every month, such as car insurance, rent for a storage unit, or maybe purchasing propane for the winter. Divide these dollar figures into monthly installments, even if you don't pay them that way.

Now, make a list of the typical monthly expenses you incur. These include groceries and fuel for your vehicles. Estimates are fine, but figure high rather than low.

Assuming you didn't miss anything, adding up all those monthly figures tells you how much needs to leave your bank account every thirty days or so. So far, so good.

Now, and I know this is going to be a huge pain, I want you to keep track of every single purchase you make in a month. I mean EVERYTHING, from the coffee you buy on your way to work to the candy bar at the office vending machine to the impulse movie rental when you see *Rocky XIV* was just released. Yes, even the quarter you give your daughter so she can buy candy at the dollar store machine should be noted. Keep a small notebook with you and write down every single expenditure. Paper clip any receipts to the back of the notebook, just in case you forget to write down the amount.

Your list might look something like this:

10/1	Fast food coffee	$1.06
	Redbox	$1.26
10/2	Stamps at post office	$9.40
10/4	Candy bar at work	$0.75
10/6	Fast food coffee	$1.06
	Dollar store candy machine	$0.50
10/7	Magazine	$8.39
10/10	Fast food lunch	$5.24
10/11	Bag of chips	$1.25
10/13	Fast food coffee	$1.06
10/14	Money for retirement card at work	$5.00

In just two weeks, that's almost $35 that slipped right through your fingers, much of it without you even noticing it. If we take that as a rough average, that's $70 a month and $840 a year! The scary thing is, for many people that's just scratching the surface. If you buy a cup of joe at a coffee house every single day on your way to work, that's probably running you close to $15 to $20 a month alone. Grab a breakfast sandwich along with the coffee and you're probably doubling that figure.

At this point, you're probably expecting me to say that you need to eliminate all of those impulse or frivolous expenses. Well, you're partially right. One thing I firmly believe is that life should be worth living and for some folks, that means coffee. For others, it might be the occasional candy bar. What I suggest is picking one or two of those "luxuries" that cost you money every month and do away with the rest, at least for the short-term. There's nothing wrong with having a little fun in life.

REALISTIC DEBT REDUCTION

Getting rid of debt is sort of like losing weight. There are all sorts of do-it-quick schemes out there, but the reality is quite simple. If you want to lose weight, you need to burn more calories than you consume. That's it, that's all there is to it. No matter how you accomplish it, that's what it takes.

Saving money works just as simply, though in sort of the opposite way. You need to spend less money than you earn each month. However you do it, that's what it takes to have more in your wallet at the end of the month. So, if you're expecting me to share some glorious secret here, think again. There is no super-secret formula to this and anyone who tells you otherwise is simply trying to sell you something.

With that in mind, let's look at a few ways you can work toward reducing your monthly bills.

CREDIT CARDS

The bane of our existence, credit cards are all too easy to get and for many people, extremely difficult to use responsibly. Once you're in the credit card trap, it feels like a never-ending cycle. Paying nothing more than the minimum each month means it will take you forever to pay off the balance. Few people truly understand how interest is calculated and just how quickly the balance skyrockets because of it.

The first thing you can do is call customer service and see if there is any way they will reduce your interest rate. Sometimes they will, sometimes they won't, but you'll never know unless you ask. Even if it is just a temporary drop for, say, six months, that's better than nothing. Anything you can do to get that interest rate lowered means more of your payment goes toward actually reducing the balance, rather than paying interest.

Next, assuming you're like most people and you have multiple cards, make a list of all of them, going from the one with the lowest balance to the highest. Pay as much as you can possibly afford each month toward the card with the lowest balance and just the minimum on all of the others. Once that card is paid off, put the money you were paying on it toward the next one on the list, adding the funds to the minimum you were paying. It takes time, but as long as you keep at it, and also do everything in your power to not add to the balances on those cards, you'll eventually pay them off.

Once a card is paid off, either cancel the account or cut up your card to prevent you from using it further. Canceling the card may have a slight negative impact on your credit rating, but that might be what it takes to keep you from incurring more debt. I do recommend keeping one credit card on hand for emergencies, though. The key word there is *emergencies*. A new pair of shoes, no matter how great the sale is, really doesn't qualify as an emergency. Neither does a new set of wrenches, for that matter.

UTILITIES

If your energy provider offers some sort of budget billing, where your energy consumption is averaged throughout the year rather than incurring huge bills in the winter for heat or in the summer for air conditioning, take them up on it. While it doesn't necessarily save you money, it is usually much easier on the pocketbook to pay a set amount each month.

The thermostat setting is one of those little things that can lead to a lot of strife in a household. It is rare that all members of the family are absolutely comfortable at the same temperature. One person is almost always too warm and another too cold. But the less energy you consume, the less money it will cost you. In my home, we keep the thermostat set at about 65°F in the winter and 78°F in the summer. Occasionally, during periods of extreme outside temperatures, we'll adjust accordingly. We also use a wood stove for supplemental heat in the winter, and because our home is a split-level, with the lower area half underground, it stays fairly cool in the summer with just a fan moving air around. As they say, your mileage may vary.

Suffice it to say, though, if you're cold, put on a sweater. If you're warm, put on a pair of shorts. Do what you can to adjust to the temperature without moving the thermostat from a more energy-conserving setting. A programmable thermostat can be a great investment, too. In the summer, let it stay a little warmer, programming the thermostat to cool off the house about an hour before you get home. Same goes with the heat in the winter. Closing the curtains in the summer can also help to keep the house cooler. Open them in the winter to allow the sun to warm things up throughout the day.

It sounds like a no-brainer, but turn off lights, TVs, radios, and other electronics when you're not using them. Not only is it wasting energy, it is costing you money keeping those things running all the time. Many devices, such as microwave ovens and DVD players, still use some energy even when they're not in use. Some folks put devices like these on power strips and turn off the strip when the devices aren't needed. The trickle charge isn't much for each device, but it adds up over time. Every little bit helps when you're trying to reduce expenses.

Keeping your refrigerator and freezer full helps reduce the energy needed to keep those things cool. If nothing else, consider adding jugs of water, which not only helps with the energy consumption but adds to your water storage.

Speaking of water, that's a precious resource that should not be squandered or wasted. If you are on city sewer and water, and thus have a regular water bill, look at ways you can reduce your usage. Limit showers to five minutes, if possible. Easier said than done, I know, especially if you have teenagers. Make sure family members turn off faucets while brushing their teeth, rather than just letting the water (and your money) go right down the drain. Set up a rain catchment system so you can use that instead of your hose to water plants and such. With toilets, consider the following mantra: "If it's yellow, let it mellow. If it's brown, flush it down." Even with low-flow toilets, each flush uses a considerable amount of water.

Look at how you do laundry and consider ways to reduce expenses there. When the weather is nice, hang laundry to dry outside rather than using the dryer. Bath towels really don't need to be washed after every shower. If you did it right, you're clean when you get out of the tub so all you're doing is wiping off clean water. Hang the towel to dry and use it again tomorrow. In our house, we struggle with dish towels. Our kids grab a new towel from the drawer all the time, rather than using the one hanging from the oven handle. Dry dishes, they'll use a new towel. They'll then grab a new one to dry the kitchen table after washing it. Then, they'll grab yet another to dry their hands. It is a constant battle.

Continuing with laundry, it sounds silly to ask this question, but how often do you really need to wash your pants? If you have an office job, odds are pretty good that your pants aren't getting dirty/smelly/sweaty every day. Shirts? Sure, wash them after wearing them all day. Underwear? Um, yeah, absolutely. But pants? You could probably wear them at least twice before tossing them into the clothes hamper.

TELEPHONE, INTERNET, CABLE TV

These are somewhat of a subset of the utilities category. Given that they are, when you get down to brass tacks and separate luxuries from necessities, think long and hard about how much you truly *need* them. For many of us, the Internet probably outranks our cell phones and cable TV. At least with the Internet, you can make phone calls via Skype and watch shows via Hulu and Netflix.

I would strongly advise you to examine each bill you receive for these services. Look at them closely every single month, line by line. Question any charge you don't immediately understand. More than once my wife has found charges that didn't belong and a simple call to the provider removed them.

If you suffer any sort of service outage, even if it is just the Internet going down for an hour, call your provider and request a credit to your account for that day. It probably won't be much, just a couple of dollars, but why should you pay for something you couldn't use? Keep in mind, though, your call needs to be placed the same day as the outage occurred. They usually won't go back and give you a credit for something that happened yesterday, let alone a week ago.

Bundle packages, where you lump together your landline phone, TV, and/or Internet together on one bill can indeed save you money—sometimes. Shop around to get the best price for the services you want and don't sign up for anything you don't need. My family ditched cable TV a few years ago and honestly haven't missed it much at all. My wife and I rarely had time to sit and veg in front of the TV and we certainly didn't need to use it to babysit our kids for hours on end. We've done just fine using Netflix and DVD sets from the library to keep up with our favorite shows. When a new season is released, we'll binge-watch for a few weeks and get all caught up. Plus, no commercials! On the flip side of that coin, I know a guy who spends somewhere north of $200 a month subscribing to most of the premium cable channels, yet rarely watches anything other than the Food Network, History Channel, or Lifetime. Don't ask me why, I can't make heads or tails of it either.

One trick you can try is to call your service provider and tell them you are looking to move to a different company. More often than not, they'll bend over backward to reduce your bill, sometimes with other incentives like a free premium cable channel or a higher speed for your Internet. It can't hurt to ask, right?

Many people today have ditched landline telephones completely and operate strictly off cell service. While this can save you money, provided you have a decent cell provider, I don't like the idea. See, in the event of a power outage, landline phones will often still operate, even if cell service has been disrupted. Just something to consider when making that decision.

FOOD/GROCERIES

True confession: I enjoy fast food as much as the next American. Culver's is my treat of choice as I do love me a ButterBurger. But I also recognize the fact that it costs me far more at a restaurant than it would for me to make it at home. Plus, it isn't very healthy, either. The fact is, we as a country spent obscene amounts of money on crap food. And again, I say this as a loyal American who bellies up to the fast food counter far more often than I should.

It should go without saying that home-cooked meals are cheaper and much healthier than anything you'll find in a restaurant. A pound of ground beef in my area runs about $3.75 or so. Add in the cost of hamburger buns, frozen French fries, and condiments and for a family of five, we spend around $6 or $7 total for a burger dinner at home. Compare that with an average bill of $25 or so if we ate out. Plus, we can add extra veggies to each plate at home to make things a bit healthier all around.

We'll talk more about scratch cooking in a later chapter. For right now, consider this. There is a hidden cost involved with eating meals out. When you factor in the cost of healthcare related to obesity, high blood pressure, diabetes, and other ailments that are a direct result of eating a lot of fast food, that kid's meal just got a whole lot more expensive.

With that out of the way, let's look at ways to save money at the grocery store. Coupons can help a lot, provided you use them intelligently. Just because you have a $0.75 coupon on an item doesn't always mean it is the best deal. In most cases, the generic brand is just as good as the name brand. Not always, of course, but more often than not. In fact, I've been told that some generic food items are packaged by the same companies that provide the name-brand versions. Almost identical products, just labeled differently. Only use coupons on items when the net result ends up cheaper than purchasing the generic brand.

Another thing to watch for with coupons is opportunities for *stacking*. In essence, this is when you have multiple coupons to use for the same item. For example, let's say Walgreens has a certain brand of shampoo on sale for $2.50. They may also have a coupon in their sale flyer that gets you $0.50 off, making that bottle $2. But, lo and behold, Sunday's newspaper had another coupon, this one from the manufacturer, that gets you another $0.75 off. Adding all of that together, the shampoo now costs $1.25. Not a bad deal. This is why I always suggest you get the Sunday newspaper each week. It might cost you a few dollars, but odds are pretty good you'll find enough coupons inside to offset that expense. Plus, the Sunday paper always has the best comics.

Watch for sales and stock up when the price is right. When you find a great deal on something you would normally buy anyway, grab extra. This allows you to eat tomorrow at today's prices. Keep an eye open for in-store specials and always check the clearance sections of the store. You never know what you'll find there.

Some people like to comparison shop between stores in neighboring areas. This isn't a bad plan, but you need to consider the cost of the gas, as well as your time. If a loaf of bread costs $0.25 less at a store that's 15 miles away, you'll probably burn more in fuel getting there and back than you'll save on the bread.

Convenience foods almost always cost more than you'd spend in ingredients to make them yourself. But when time is short and you need to get a meal on the table, sometimes tossing a box into the microwave is what it takes. Not the healthiest meal, nor the tastiest, but as long as you limit it to a once-in-a-while thing, shop intelligently, and, as a result of sale prices or the use of coupons, save a bit of money on the purchase, have at it.

HEALTH EXPENSES

I'm going to jump up on my soapbox just for a moment. We live in a nation where a significant percentage of the population suffers from at least one, but usually multiple, health maladies. Many of those issues are a direct result of our lifestyles. We consume chemicals that are disguised as food and then get surprised when we get sick because of it. We are obese because we don't eat right and don't exercise. We have high blood pressure, diabetes, and all manner of other ailments for which we pop pill after pill after pill. The end result? As a country, we spend millions of dollars every month on health expenses, yet we don't get any healthier.

To a degree, this is an example of Pot meeting Kettle as I'm far from the healthiest person you'll ever meet. I will readily admit I have a hard time sitting down to a meal that doesn't include meat and if you were to draw blood from my arm, odds are that Mountain Dew will come out. But as I've gotten older, I've started to do something I should have done years ago—listen to my wife. She has badgered me for years about eating better, exercising, and taking better care of my body. Given that I'm genetically predisposed to heart disease, diabetes, and a few other fun things, I've finally started to take this seriously and suggest you do the same.

My point is this. The healthier you are, the less money you'll end up spending on healthcare in the long run. Granted, we can't predict the future and you could get hit by a bus the same day you're celebrating a full year without junk food. But even if that did happen, assuming you survive the encounter, your body will be able to bounce back and heal far more quickly if you were in reasonably good health than if you ate a box of Twinkies every day for the last year.

Eating healthier and getting your heart rate up on a regular basis can work wonders for your overall health, at little to no expense. You don't need to go out and buy some fancy exercise equipment that will just end up being an interesting place to hang laundry. Go for a walk every day. Do some stretching or jog in place. Just do something to get off your butt and burn some calories. You'll thank me later.

Okay, I'm off the soapbox now, so let's talk about reducing health expenses a bit. If you're fighting massive bills from doctors and hospitals, call them. See if you're able to work out some sort of payment arrangement that will not put undue burden on your family. As long as you keep the account current with their office, they probably won't send it to a collection agency, saving you fees and possibly interest charges. Whatever you do, though, don't pay the account off with a credit card! Doing so will indeed result in interest charges being tacked on to the original balance.

RENT/MORTGAGE

You have to live somewhere and unless you're still living with your parents, odds are your housing arrangement is costing you money. If you pay rent, talk to your landlord about trading some maintenance work for a reduction in your rent. Some landlords would jump at the opportunity to have someone on site take care of shoveling snow in the winter and maintaining flower beds in the summer in exchange for, say, $100 off your rent each month. Just make sure you are physically able to do the work you are promising and keep up your end of the bargain.

You might also offer to help clean out units when people move, painting the walls and that sort of stuff. While this probably wouldn't be an each-and-every month deal, it could still save you some dough.

If you pay a mortgage rather than rent, the bank certainly isn't going to be interested in your offering to mow your own lawn in exchange for reducing your payment each month. In fact, about the only way you'll be able to reduce your mortgage payment is to refinance, which isn't something you'd be able to do very often. It is worth considering, though, if you've been in the home for several years and your credit is good enough to qualify for a lower interest rate. Talk to your lender about that possibility.

What I will recommend to homeowners is this—pay as much as you can comfortably afford each month in addition to your required payment. Even as little as $100 extra on the principle every month will significantly reduce the amount of time you'll be making those payments.

IS DEBT CONSOLIDATION A GOOD IDEA?

If you own your home, one possible way to help get out from under debt is to take out a home equity loan for the purpose of debt consolidation. At a very basic level, what you're doing is borrowing money from the bank, using your home as collateral, and using the funds to pay off several of your debts at once. On the surface, it sounds like a win-win. But, I would caution you against doing this unless it becomes an absolute necessity. Most of your debts are what we call *unsecured*. This means you put up no collateral when you opened the line of credit. A credit card is a great example. If you end up not paying the balance, they can certainly sue you for it but they can't come after your home.

By taking out an equity loan to pay the credit card, the amount owed is now *secured*. If you don't make the payments on that loan, the bank can and will come after your home.

Food for thought.

CREDIT MANAGEMENT

Avoid ever maxing out a credit card as this is a big red flag for creditors. Keep the balances low if you can't pay them off each month. At the same time, though, and I know this sounds counterintuitive, you need to use credit to build up your credit score. Paying cash for everything and never using a credit card or installment loan doesn't provide any positive information to the credit bureaus. If you're nothing but a blank slate to them, you aren't going to enjoy any sort of stellar credit score and should the time come you need to open a line of credit, you won't qualify for the most favorable terms.

It should go without saying, but go through each billing statement every month and make sure everything is accurate. On top of checking for errors, be sure you understand what each charge is for, especially when it comes to utility accounts like cell phones and Internet services. Those companies in particular are notorious for adding fees and charges for services you didn't order or that don't apply to your account. Should you find something you don't understand or you believe to be an error, contact the company immediately to get it handled.

The takeaway here is that you need to pay attention to your credit and how it affects other areas of your life. Having the means to pay your typical living expenses in cash each month is great, but consider the fact that at some point down the road, whether you like it or not, you may just need to apply for a loan. Managing credit effectively will go a long way toward improving your overall financial existence.

CREDIT SCORE

In the banking world, you *are* your credit score. That number represents your reliability when it comes to debt repayment, and it's also an indicator of your overall responsibility. It affects many areas of your life, from determining whether you qualify for a loan to the loan terms you might receive and even your rates for insurance. The higher your credit score, the better the rates and terms you'll receive.

There are three major credit bureaus in the United States: Experian, TransUnion, and Equifax. Each of them has a file with your name all over it, whether you like it or not. This file, called a credit report, is supposed to contain an accurate documentation of your repayment history. I say it is *supposed to* because they aren't always 100 percent correct.

Now, persons far smarter than me have attempted to determine exactly how a credit score is generated. We know, for example, that late payments tend to decrease your score and being responsible with your debt load increases your score. However, when it comes to calculating the exact number, well, it is sort of a mystery.

Credit scores range from 300–850; the higher the better. There are gray areas when it comes to what's good versus merely acceptable credit. Lenders have their own guidelines. However, as a general rule of thumb, a score of 740 and up is considered excellent, and those individuals usually enjoy the most favorable rates and terms. A score of 680–740 is still considered pretty good. The rates extended won't be quite as awesome as those in the upper bracket, but lenders aren't going to put you over a barrel, either. The next level down, 620–680, is the lowest rung still considered acceptable by most lenders. You'll still likely get approved, all other factors being equal, but the terms aren't going to be stellar. The further down you go from there, the less likely you'll even be approved for credit, let alone see terms that are close to acceptable.

These ranges are ballpark figures. Every lender is slightly different in terms of what they consider good versus average credit scores.

NAVIGATING CREDIT REPORTS

It is important to review your credit report on a regular basis. This might be the only way you'll ever learn of errors on it as well as see indications of fraud or identity theft. Fortunately, getting a copy of your credit report is very easy. The Fair Credit Reporting Act (FCRA) requires the three credit bureaus to provide, upon request, one copy of their credit report, free of charge, to each consumer once a year. The report may be ordered via one of three ways:

Online: Visit www.annualcreditreport.com. Be wary of look-alike websites with similar domain names. This one is the only one set up as a result of the FCRA. There are a lot of scam sites out there that will either charge you or just outright steal your information. Ordering your report online grants you immediate access to it.

Mail: Fill out the form entitled Annual Credit Report Request, found on the Annual Credit Report website, then mail it to:

Annual Credit Report Request Service

P.O. Box 105281

Atlanta, GA 30348-5281

Response time is about two weeks from when the request is received.

Telephone: Call 1-877-322-8228 and order your report. As with mailing, it will take about two weeks to get your report.

It is important to rely upon one of these methods, rather than contacting the credit bureaus directly. The website, mailing address, and phone number listed above are the only ways to obtain your free copy each calendar year. The credit bureaus are likely going to charge you if you go directly through them.

You are entitled to one copy from each bureau every twelve months. Rather than ordering all three at once, I suggest you stagger the requests and order one from a different bureau every four months. This allows you to react more quickly in the event you do see something amiss on the report.

CREDIT REPORT VS. CREDIT SCORE

Obtaining a copy of your credit report is a fairly straightforward process. Getting your own credit score, though, is a whole other ball game. See, the score won't be printed on the credit report. The credit bureaus keep those scores locked up tighter than a clam with lockjaw. You can request a copy of your credit score from each of the three bureaus, but they'll charge you a fee for providing it.

Some credit card companies have the means in place to provide their customers with their credit scores. This is a great option for many people, provided you can be responsible with the credit card itself. As this is an option that comes and goes with different companies, you'll have to do your own research to find which ones currently offer it.

REPORTING INACCURACIES

Go through each credit report line by line, even including your name, your address, and all of your other identifying information. The balances listed for each account will probably not be accurate right down to the penny as there is a lag between when you make a payment and when that payment is reported to the credit bureau. However, look for accounts that are listed as open, even though you closed them years ago, or accounts that are listed as delinquent even though you're up to date on all payments.

Be sure to check for any accounts you weren't aware of as these are indicators of possible fraud. Bear in mind, though, that the names listed as account holders may differ slightly from the ones which are familiar to you. Banks change names from time to time.

Should you find something amiss on your credit report, you need to get it handled as soon as possible. These things take time, so the faster you act, the sooner it can get fixed. Every credit report will have instructions on how to report possible errors, which will need to be reported in writing directly to the credit bureau. They have 30 days or so to investigate the matter and respond back to you. Typically, what will happen is the credit bureau will contact the person or entity (both are considered to be Credit Reporting Agencies, or CRAs) that originally reported the information. The bureau will notify them of the dispute and pass along the information you've provided on the matter. The CRA must conduct an investigation and report the findings back to the credit bureau.

If the CRA provides documentation that the information is valid and correct, it stays on your credit report. However, if they are unable to provide that documentation, the information is changed or deleted on your credit report.

Of course, you could also skip the credit bureau and contact the CRA directly about your dispute. Depending upon the circumstances, this may or may not speed up the process. It is one thing if you are dealing with a large company that likely has processes in place for dealing with disputes and knows how to handle such matters efficiently. It's another thing entirely if you're dealing with a landlord or some other relatively small-time operation.

INCREASE YOUR CREDIT SCORE

While we might not know how to calculate our own credit scores precisely, we do know of several factors that come into play to increase the number.

PAYMENT HISTORY. First and foremost, strive to make all of your payments on time, every time. Every late payment counts against you and payments that are completely missed count even more. Pay close attention to due dates and remember that even just paying the minimum is far better than not paying anything at all.

I would venture a guess that the vast majority of bills you have each month can be paid online. Plus, a lot of companies today allow you to schedule payments ahead of time. This can be a great option, provided you are certain the funds will be in your account when the payment is due.

For those who, whether by necessity or preference, still wish to mail checks, here's a system we used successfully for years. Once a week, sit down with all of the bills that came in the mail. Write out the checks and get the payment ready to mail for each one, sealing the envelope and everything. On the outside of the envelope, where your return address goes, write in the date by which the payment must be mailed, being sure to allow plenty of time for it to arrive before the deadline. Keep all of these payments clipped together on the fridge in the order they must be mailed, with the payment due first on top. Check the stack every day or so and mail out the payments as needed, covering your written "mail by" date with a return address label.

Sometimes, we get into trouble because we have several accounts that all require payment at nearly the same time each month. If that's the case for you, call your credit card companies and see if you can adjust the due date for your account. I'm not talking about a one-time deal, but permanently. If you have a bunch of stuff that is always due on or near the 20th of the month, maybe get one or two of them moved to the 10th to space things out.

PAYMENT AMOUNTS. Whenever possible, pay your balance due in full each month. Doing so not only avoids your having to pay interest charges but indicates responsible debt management, which increases your credit score. If you have fallen behind a bit and can't pay the entire balance on a credit card, try to at least pay off any new charges plus the interest fee for the month. This will prevent your balance from growing each month and help you to get a better handle on the account.

Always pay as much as you can afford on each account every month. Sometimes that won't be a whole lot, but do what you can to pay off balances quickly.

HISTORICAL ACCOUNTS. Sometimes when we finally pay off an account, we're tempted to close it completely so as to avoid getting into further trouble. That's not the worst idea in the world. But consider keeping at least one old account open. Use it from time to time, making small purchases and paying the balance in full when the bill arrives. This helps you to build a positive history of debt management.

DIVERSIFY YOUR DEBTS. Creditors like to see that you know how to handle different types of debt. As situations warrant, diversify your debts so as to include installment loans, credit cards, and a mortgage. I'm not suggesting you run out and buy a new set of furniture for the sole purpose of trying to increase your credit score! But, if given the option of using a credit card or an installment loan, go with the one that not only gives you the most favorable terms but is one you might not have used in the last few years.

DEBT RATIO. Ideally, your credit debt should be around 30 percent of your net income. This figure does not include mortgage payments. Debt ratios are a key figure in determining whether you'll get approved for a loan or line of credit. Creditors want to see that you not only have the necessary income to pay the loan, but that enough of that income is free to be used for the payments.

BRINGING IN EXTRA INCOME

The flip side to reducing expenses is to increase your income. The more money you have coming in, the less of an impact debt will have on you. You'll be able to pay off bills more quickly, and, hopefully, have some fun money left over. There are several possibilities to consider.

TURN JUNK INTO TREASURE

A good friend of mine has always been rather artistic and knows her way around a toolbox. In the last few years, she's been making pretty decent extra income refurbishing old furniture. She'll either buy it cheap at a rummage sale or grab it for nothing on trash day. A new coat of paint, some new hardware, and she sells it online for a tidy profit.

Along these same lines is buying stuff on the cheap and reselling it elsewhere without improving upon it. If you have an eye for bargains and know the market for certain types of items, you can sometimes find great deals at thrift stores, flea markets, and garage sales, then sell the items to collectors and such online.

LAWN CARE

If you, or perhaps your resident teenager, have the time and equipment, you might bring in some extra money mowing lawns, weeding garden beds, and performing other relatively simple lawn care chores. In some areas, people make a fairly substantial income cleaning up dog waste from yards. Not a fun job, of course, but if you're willing to do it and someone else is willing to pay you for it, why not? The beauty of this sort of work is you can usually set your own schedule and work it in around your day job and other commitments. I would caution you, though, to get paid immediately upon rendering the service. More than one enterprising person has been left holding the proverbial bag.

Related to this is snow removal in the winter. Many homeowners would love the opportunity to spend a few bucks for a cleared driveway. If you have a snow blower, all the better. We used to have a guy in our neighborhood who, after every major snowstorm, would go down the street and offer to take care of driveways and sidewalks for a very modest fee.

NEWSPAPER DELIVERY

Once the realm of preteen boys riding bicycles in the wee hours of the morning, paper routes today are increasingly taken over by adults. This is another part-time gig that doesn't typically interfere with most day jobs. Pay depends on the size of the route but is often fairly lucrative, given that the actual labor involved is minimal. In most communities, there are as many opportunities for routes as there are different papers needing to be delivered. Usually, there is at least one daily newspaper and then there will be what I call the "local fish wrap," which is the free paper consisting mostly of classified ads. That one usually comes out only once or twice a week.

WRITING

There are many opportunities to make some extra money writing, both online and on site. While certainly not for the thin-skinned, submitting articles to magazines and even newspapers presents the potential for decent money. A full discussion of this line of work is well beyond the scope of this book. If this is an area of interest to you, I would suggest you start with borrowing a recent edition of *Writer's Market* from your library. Not only does it list thousands of publications seeking work, but there are always several very informative articles in each edition. Be warned, though. As a very close friend of mine has told me, "Writing is a great way to get rich... but a poor way to make a living." Unless you miraculously land a six-figure deal on a novel, complete with film studios bidding for the movie rights, consider this supplemental income at best.

RECYCLING

More and more people have jumped on this opportunity, but there is still money to be made if you're quick and know what you're doing. If you have a truck and a strong back, you can make some decent money hauling old appliances and other scrap metal to recycling outfits. It isn't going to amount to a ton of money each and every week, but if you're already out driving your truck to and from work each day, keep your eyes open. Let the junk accumulate in your truck bed until you have enough to make it worth the trip to the recycler. I would warn you, though, to avoid aluminum cans that have been placed at the end of the driveway in recycle bins. In some areas, I've heard taking them is treated as theft from the trash hauler. Be forewarned.

There are many other ways you can bring in a few extra bucks each month. Often, something you enjoy as a hobby can turn into a decent sideline, such as working on engines or being a seamstress. Ask your family and friends to help you get the word out. Use free online sources such as Craigslist, too. If you do good work, those who are willing to pay for it will find their way to you.

CHAPTER 3

CURRENCY

When we talk about investments that could mitigate an economic collapse, a key element to remember is *diversification*. Don't put all your eggs in one basket and rely solely upon any one particular investment. By spreading the wealth, so to speak, you are less likely to be left empty-handed if the dollar crashes.

In this chapter, we're going to talk about what currency is and what it isn't, then discuss currencies from around the world that might be worth your investment.

WHAT IS CURRENCY?

Currency developed as a convenient way to buy and sell goods. Using a few seashells or primitive coins was a whole lot easier than carrying around chickens and pelts all the time. Currency has historically come in two different types: commodity currency and fiat currency.

COMMODITY CURRENCY

Essentially, commodity currency is that which has inherent value. By that, I mean the item being used as currency is, in and of itself, valuable to some degree. For example, over the years things like tobacco, salt, and peppercorns have been used as money. In addition to being traded in exchange for other goods, these things could also be used by those who owned them. Other commodity items might not have practical use but possess significant beauty, such as certain kinds of seashells.

In many ways, commodity currency usage is very similar to barter systems. You are trading one useful item for another. The basic difference between a barter exchange system and a commodity currency system is that with the latter, it is typically a single specific item that becomes the currency of choice for everyone. For example, it is forbidden for inmates in the United States prison system to possess money. Any purchases made at the commissary are paid for using accounts set up for each inmate. The accounts have funds added to them either through the money the inmate earns working in the prison or by contributions from family and friends. For a long time, though, cigarettes were used as a form of commodity currency between inmates. A pack of smokes could ensure your protection for a period of time, for instance. You have, no doubt, seen that sort of scene played out in any number of movies.

When prisons outlawed smoking, something else had to take the place of that currency. Believe it or not, the commodity of choice became mackerel. A package of mackerel has a fairly consistent price and is small enough to be easily used as currency. While it has inherent value as it could be consumed, by and large it is just used as money to buy goods and services between inmates.

Of course, another example of commodity currency is gold or silver coins. Usually, these are minted by division of the government and stamped or marked in some way to note the weight and purity of the coin. While the actual value of the gold or silver might fluctuate on a regular basis, those who use these coins as currency more or less agree on a fixed value, at least for periods of time. The difference between commodity currency like gold coins and *fiat currency*, which we'll discuss next, is that if you were to melt down the gold, it retains its value.

Back in the days when Europeans were first settling in North America, many Native American tribes used *wampum* as a form of currency. Today, we might think of that term as a sort of catch-all for any type of trinkets that were traded, but it actually refers to a rather specific item. Wampum consisted of certain types of mollusk shells that had been transformed by hand into beads. These were then strung on cordage and used as currency. Because of the work involved in turning the shells into beads, they were somewhat rare. One couldn't just head to the seashore and grab a handful of shells to trade. While these beads may not have been useful in a practical sense, certainly not like salt or tobacco, they held value because of their beauty and the work involved in producing them. The problem came when Europeans began using the same wampum, though. Because they had access to tools, Europeans could produce far more beads and at a faster rate, which ended up flooding the market, so to speak, and caused the wampum to decrease in value.

Incidentally, wampum is where the slang terms *shelling out* and *clams* as related to money originated.

FIAT CURRENCY

The word *fiat* in this sense does not refer to a type of automobile but rather an order or decree. Fiat currency is essentially some type of token or certificate that the governing body has issued some sort of value. The dollars in your wallet are a great example. The federal government has told us, and we all sort of agreed, that this piece of paper bearing the image of George Washington has the value of one United States dollar. In and of itself, the dollar has no intrinsic value. You can't eat it, drink it, smoke it, or use it in any real way other than trading it for things you want or need.

Once upon a time, our paper money was commodity-based. A government would mint coins using precious metals, such as silver or gold, and the paper money would be worth a set amount of those coins. A paper dollar could get you one dollar's worth of gold or silver, for example. Today, not so much. Fiat currency is, for all intents and purposes, faith-based. We all just sort of agree to use these certain pieces of paper to conduct our financial transactions.

This is where the problem lies because, well, if people lose faith in the dollar, it loses value. Sort of like how Tinker Bell could die if the audience doesn't clap their hands really, really loudly.

The other problem with fiat money is that any currency is, in a way, tied to its own rarity. Just like anything else, supply versus demand comes into play. The more widgets there are in the world, and the easier it is to obtain them, the less value they hold. I mean, let's say someone came up to you and asked if you'd trade one of your apples for a handful of dust bunnies. On top of wondering just where they'd misplaced their tin foil beanie, you'd probably think, "Why would I do that? I have plenty of my own dust bunnies behind the couch!" Dust bunnies are obviously too common to be ever considered any form of currency. Now, extrapolate that admittedly silly example to the federal government. The more dollars in print, the more common they are and thus the less value they hold.

Too many dollars in circulation plus a sudden reduction in faith in them could result in a collapse that all the clapping in the world isn't going to remedy.

"SAFE" WORLD CURRENCIES

Historically, in times of economic strife within a country, citizens have turned to foreign currencies as a substitute for their own. This happens when the domestic currency is no longer considered stable, yet people need some form of money to continue conducting business. The upside to investing in one or more foreign currencies is you'll have money on hand to buy the things you need should the dollar collapse.

The downside, though, is there's no way to know for certain which, if any, foreign currencies will become commonly used should such a collapse come to pass. In times past, the foreign currency often used was one that originated in a neighboring country. This was perhaps due to geography or familiarity more than anything else.

Fortunately, in today's ever-smaller world, we have many choices for world currencies in which we could invest. There are currency exchanges in every large city and many small suburbs. There are several world currencies that have a history of stability and would make for feasible alternatives to the US dollar, should it collapse.

Currency	2008	2009	2010	2011	2012	2013
EUROPE						
British Pound	$0.57	$0.67	$0.67	$0.65	$0.66	$0.67
Swiss Franc	$1.13	$1.13	$1.09	$0.92	$0.98	$0.96
Euro	$0.71	$0.75	$0.79	$0.75	$0.81	$0.78
Norwegian Krone	$5.87	$6.55	$6.29	$5.84	$6.06	$6.12
THE AMERICAS						
Canadian Dollar	$1.11	$1.19	$1.07	$1.02	$1.04	$1.07
Cayman Dollar	$0.87	$0.86	$0.87	$0.87	$0.87	$0.87
Mexican Peso	$11.61	$15.06	$13.15	$12.94	$13.70	$13.28
ASIA						
China Yuan	$7.24	$7.12	$7.05	$6.73	$6.57	$6.45
Hong Kong Dollar	$8.09	$9.06	$8.08	$8.10	$8.07	$8.07
Singapore Dollar	$1.47	$1.51	$1.42	$1.31	$1.30	$1.30
AUSTRALIA						
Australian Dollar	$1.25	$1.33	$1.13	$1.01	$1.01	$1.08

source: www.irs.gov

This chart shows the annual mean buying power for the dollar against different world currencies from 2008–2013. For example, on this chart the Euro has lost value against the dollar—in 2008 US$1 only bought you €0.71 whereas in 2013 US$1 purchased €0.78.

SWISS FRANC

Currently, the Swiss franc is legal tender in only two countries—Switzerland and Liechtenstein. Despite this fact, the franc is considered one of the most stable currencies in the world. Much of this reputation stems from the overall stability of the Swiss government. With its long-standing neutral stance on the world stage, Switzerland is able to avoid many of the issues that plague other countries, such as entering into conflicts that could result in serious economic consequences.

The Swiss banking system is largely considered one of the safest in the world. This is why you often hear about the "Swiss bank account" mentioned in novels and movies. Not only are accounts afforded a high degree of privacy, the deposits aren't likely to be lost in some sort of bank collapse.

NORWEGIAN KRONE

Because Norway doesn't belong to the European Union, it is autonomous from the countries around it. Also, Norway has far more assets than debts. Norway is rather resource-rich, particularly with oil. The krone is not tied to any other currency, meaning it cannot be devalued as a result of some other country's financial misfortune.

Historically, the krone has always been very strong, particularly when compared to the US dollar. It is accepted as currency in Norway, of course, as well as in many border towns in Finland and Sweden.

CANADIAN DOLLAR

Like Norway, Canada has tremendous amounts of natural resources, especially oil and uranium. Plus, Americans, particularly those who live in the northern parts of the US, have some moderate familiarity with Canadian currency.

However, Canada is very much tied to the US economy, due to the large amount of imports they receive from us. Should the US dollar collapse, it may end up taking the Canadian dollar with it, at least to a degree.

AUSTRALIAN DOLLAR

Australia is yet another resource-rich country (are you seeing a theme, yet?). It is the world's third-largest producer of gold. They have also proven to be very proactive in the face of economic downturns and, as a result, are fairly stable financially.

However, Australia is also heavily tied to China, one of their chief commodity customers. Should that relationship deteriorate, there would likely be severe economic ramifications.

SING DOLLAR

Singapore is widely recognized as one of the least corrupt nations on the planet. As a result, its banking system is seen as very stable. On top of that, Singapore is one of the world's financial hubs as well as a top oil-refining center. Its main port is one of the busiest in the world. Suffice it to say, there's a lot of business going on in this country of less than 300 square miles.

The downside of the Sing dollar is its relative obscurity to Americans. Few average citizens have likely even seen a Sing dollar, let alone recognize it when it is placed in front of them.

Whether we're talking about krones, gold nuggets, or mackerels, recognize the very real possibility that any particular form of currency could fall apart at some point down the road. While I encourage you to consider investing in some form of foreign currency, don't make that your only investment.

"RISKY" WORLD CURRENCIES

As you research different currencies in which to invest, you'll come across the term *pegged*, usually referring to a certain currency being pegged to the US dollar. What this means is the exchange rate is fixed and does not fluctuate. For example, the Netherlands Antillean guilder is currently pegged at US$1.79. No matter what happens in the financial markets, that rate doesn't change.

While that makes things easier in some ways, it isn't ideal at all when we're talking about investing in foreign currencies as a hedge against a possible currency collapse in the United States. If the US dollar tanks, it may likely take these pegged currencies down as well, at least in terms of our use of them as replacement currency. Therefore, avoid pegged currencies.

The euro is currently the most heavily used currency in the world other than the US dollar. It is seen as generally stable. These two factors alone would seem to indicate it is a viable alternative currency. However, the euro suffers from some of the same problems as the dollar. Chiefly, some of the nations that invest in the euro are economically weak or have large deficits. This causes the value of the euro to drop.

The Chinese yuan or renminbi is another currency that is somewhat risky. You'll see the terms *renminbi* and *yuan* sometimes used interchangeably, but they do have distinct meanings. Renminbi is the name of the overall currency; and the yuan is the unit measurement. The renminbi was pegged to the US dollar until 2005. Since then, it has floated a bit in value as compared to other world currencies. For our purposes, one of the chief reasons to avoid it as an investment is simply because many people in America will shy away from using Chinese currency, for right or wrong reasons.

EMERGING CURRENCIES AND OPEN SOURCE/CRYPTOCURRENCY

Given how pervasive technology has become in our lives, it stands to reason forms of electronic currency have developed. Perhaps the best known of these so-called cryptocurrencies is Bitcoin, though there are several others out there, with more likely on the way. At the most basic level, cryptocurrency consists of bits of electronic data that is traded back and forth.

The jury is still out, so to speak, on whether Bitcoin and other cryptocurrencies are going to take the place of paper money. A growing number of businesses are accepting them as payment. However, I cannot recommend it as a viable currency to stockpile in the event the US dollar collapses. The thing is, cryptocurrencies are contingent upon computer networks working flawlessly. If the grid were to go down, you'd have no way to access the funds. By their very nature, cryptocurrencies need a working power grid to be traded.

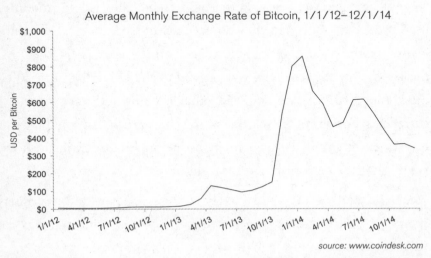

Average Monthly Exchange Rate of Bitcoin, 1/1/12–12/1/14

source: www.coindesk.com

Bitcoin proved to be one of the most exciting investment opportunities of the last several years. That being said, its value has been plummeting from a staggering peak in early 2014. That peak was due to hype more than any economic factors, so Bitcoin's long-term investment potential is still very much up in the air.

That said, there may be investment value in cryptocurrencies for some people. Bitcoin and some of the others have seen huge swings in value, going from $0.10 a "bit" to thousands of dollars. If you like taking risks and can afford to lose money if things don't go your way, there is a chance to make a significant return on investment with cryptocurrencies. Just be sure to cash out and convert your earnings to something more stable.

PURCHASING AND TRADING FOREIGN CURRENCIES

When it comes to purchasing foreign currency, bear in mind that your goal is to have the actual paper money in hand. I know that sounds obvious, but it is an important distinction to make as you research local options. Many investment companies are very willing to invest your funds in other currencies, but those transactions happen only on paper or a computer screen. Having a few thousand dollars in an online account won't do you much good if you can't access it due to business closures and such.

Many banks, certainly all of the major ones, can order foreign currencies for you. Exchange rates change daily but are generally favorable when compared to other options. Most banks won't order coins, though, only paper money. Not a huge issue in most cases, but it is something to bear in mind. Typically, this isn't something you can just walk in and handle on the spot. Your best bet is to call your local bank branch and ask about their procedures for currency exchanges. Often, you can place your order online and pick up the currency at your local branch within a couple of days.

If you belong to a travel club like AAA, they usually offer currency exchanges as well. You may end up paying a bit more compared to banks due to shipping charges. However, if the amount you're exchanging is high enough, some of them will waive those fees.

A third option is a local currency exchange company. You can find these businesses in many moderate to large cities. They will have the most common world currencies immediately available, though the exchange rates may not be quite as nice as you'd find elsewhere.

Of course, should you find yourself traveling through a country whose currency you find favorable, you'll be able to trade your US dollars for the local wampum at hotels, airports, and other locations. The exchange rates, though, are likely to be rather steep when compared to the options outlined above.

You'll notice I've mentioned *exchange rates* several times. This refers to the actual cost to you for obtaining the foreign currency. For example, as I write this, the exchange rate for Swiss francs is about US$1.09. This means, it will cost me $1.09 of American money to buy one franc. This is slightly higher than the rate I'll see quoted in the newspapers and currency trading websites. The reason for this disparity is that the market rates you'll find published are for *interbank* transactions typically amounting to $1 million or more per transaction. The rates offered to us normal folks are going to be a little higher. Continuing with our Swiss franc example, the interbank exchange rate right now is US$1.03, a whopping difference of US$0.06.

Exchange rates change every day and will differ a bit between businesses. When it comes time to pull the trigger and purchase foreign currency, shop around for the best rate, taking into account any additional fees, such as the cost of shipping the currency to you.

Also worth noting are warnings you'll see from agencies like the Better Business Bureau about currency investment scams. There are shady individuals out there who'll proclaim you can make millions in trading foreign currencies. While there is *some* money to be made by playing these markets, like anything else in life, if it sounds too good to be true, it probably is. However, these sorts of investment deals, whether legit or fraud, aren't the focus of our discussion here. What we're doing is buying foreign currency to be used in the event of US dollar collapse. We're not buying the currency in hopes of trading it back later at a profit. We're setting it aside for the proverbial rainy day.

SAFELY STORING PAPER CURRENCY

While we'll get into details later on storing your investments in a secure manner at home, let's talk just for a bit about paper currency. Unlike precious metals and commodities, paper money tends to be a bit fragile. Granted, for most of us, cash doesn't sit around long enough to where storing it becomes problematic. We're not talking about your day-to-day money, though, but paper currency you're planning to store long-term.

Perhaps the best way to store paper money long-term is to start with Mylar pouches. You can find these pouches online at Amazon and elsewhere; just search for "currency sleeves" and you'll find dozens of options. They come in different sizes because, well, money isn't the same size all over the world. Currency sleeves aren't very expensive unless you want to pop for the museum-grade varieties.

These sleeves come in a few different configurations, too. You can buy them as single pouches, which would then be stacked upright into a box or safe of some sort. They also come in sheets with convenient holes for use in three-ring binders. The third option, also the most expensive, is to buy a specially designed currency wallet or album. Any of these are perfectly fine, just base your decision on how and where you plan on storing the currency.

One word of caution, though. When selecting the currency sleeve, be sure it is truly made of Mylar and not some other sort of plastic.

Lesser-grade currency sleeves will not only yellow and crack over time, they'll leach chemicals onto the currency, leading to damage. Of course, while we're not truly concerned about keeping the paper currency in mint condition, we want to avoid any possibility of rendering it useless over time.

Whether you opt for standalone sleeves or the type that are kept in a binder, store the currency in a cool, dry, dark location. Naturally, inside a safe would be best, both for keeping the money secure as well as protected from damage. If that's not a viable option for you, keeping it high up on a bookshelf, well away from prying eyes as well as sunlight or possible flooding, should work fine.

CHAPTER 4

PRECIOUS METALS AND MINERALS

For what seems like forever, shiny stuff has caught man's eye. We love those little trinkets and baubles that sparkle. Outside of some of the more modern industrial applications, most of these precious metals and such are really worthless in a practical sense. You can't eat gold. While silver appears to have at least some medicinal properties, it isn't going to slake your thirst. Diamonds aren't going to be of much help when it comes to defending you and your family from looters and other ne'er do wells. Lead would likely be a far better choice for that, though I'd hardly consider it a precious metal.

Yet, for all that, gold and silver, along with diamonds and other gems, have been sought after and fought over since time out of mind. But, are they worth considering for end-of-the-world investment?

When we talk about precious metals, generally speaking we're referring to gold and silver above all others. These are the most recognizable and most commonly available. There are others, of course, including palladium and platinum.

GOLD

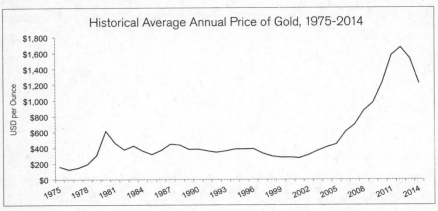

Historical Average Annual Price of Gold, 1975-2014

source: www.nma.org

The value of gold skyrocketed throughout the economic downturn that began in 2008. As the economy has improved, the price of gold has started to return to more normal levels. But gold has proven to be one of the wisest investment vehicles in the event of impending economic turmoil.

Why is gold so valuable? There are several reasons, actually. Gold is fairly easy to melt and mold into coins and jewelry, particularly in comparison to other metals like platinum. It doesn't tarnish or lose its luster over time. Gold is fairly rare, yet not impossible to find. It also stands out from all of the other elemental contenders because, interestingly enough, it is the only one that is beautifully golden in color. All other metals are either silvery or green.

Today, we have all sorts of industrial uses for gold, most of them involving electronics, as gold is a marvelous conductor. But, for eons, it was valued simply because of its beauty, ease of molding, and relative rarity.

The downside to gold, at least from a stockpiling perspective, is that it is quite heavy. You know those scenes in the movies where a thief grabs a bunch of gold bars and stuffs them in his pockets, then runs out the door or climbs up the side of a building? Yeah, not likely. A typical gold bar, like the kind depicted in the movies as being transferred between banks and such, weighs in at around 27 pounds. Gold, like other precious metals, is measured in troy ounces. One troy ounce weighs exactly 31.1034768 grams, which converts to 1.097142857143 ounces in our standard units of measure here in the United States.

Gold is also measured by purity, denoted in karats. This figure is determined by the formula:

$$K = 24 \times M_g / M_m$$

K stands for karat, naturally. M_g is the mass of pure gold in the material, and M_m is the total mass of the object. Therefore, when we say something is 24-karat gold, it is about as pure gold as we're going to get. Anything less is actually an alloy—gold combined with another metal. This is typically done due to gold's softness. Adding another metal strengthens the object. One of the most common gold alloys is 18-karat, which is 18 parts gold and 6 parts some other metal. In other words, 18K means the object is 75 percent pure gold and 25 percent something else.

Gold, when purchased, comes in a few different forms. There is jewelry, of course, available in just about any sizeable town from coast to coast. For collectors and investors, gold can be purchased as bullion coins or bars.

The absolute best ways to determine if a given item is truly gold is to either buy it from a reputable dealer or take it to a jeweler for appraisal. But that might not be an option, depending on the situation.

Authentic gold jewelry is always stamped somewhere with the purity level; again, as noted above, this will be in karat weight. It may also or alternatively be shown as a numeral indicating "fineness," noted as 1–999 (the higher the number, the higher the purity).

As you're looking for that notation on the necklace or ring, examine the item for wear marks in places where it would typically rub against the body. If you see another color of metal peeking through on those areas, the item is just gold-plated and certainly not anything approaching pure gold.

Use a strong magnet and see if the jewelry sticks to or is attracted to it. Gold is not magnetic.

One more way you can test for relative purity at home is a bit complicated, but doable if you have the right equipment on hand.

Nitric acid is what jewelers have used in the past to test gold. It isn't impossible to find but it is a dangerous chemical, so be careful with it. Let me stress that a bit more. *Do not engage in this sort of testing until you are equipped with the proper safety gear and know full well the dangers of using nitric acid, including the risks of breathing in fumes.*

Place the object to be tested into a small stainless steel bowl or cup. One drop of the nitric acid on the object is all it takes. Give it a minute or two and check for any reaction. If the object is indeed gold, nothing will happen other than perhaps a bit of dirt or grime having been removed where the acid hit the gold. Any other reaction, such as the acid turning green or a milky color indicates the object is not gold.

WHAT ABOUT THE "BITE" TEST?

In countless old movies, especially westerns, people will bite a gold coin to see if it is real. Gold is a soft metal and, at least in theory, if you're able to substantially dent the item with your teeth, it is probably gold. Out here in the real world where we don't rely on getting all of our factual information from Hollywood, don't bite coins, necklaces, bracelets, and other metal objects. First, you could damage your teeth, which is no fun for anyone. Second, if the item is counterfeit, it may have been made with another soft metal like lead, which would give your test a "false positive" result.

While there are indeed gold coins, they aren't minted for use as normal currency. Instead, they are produced primarily for investors. Among the most well-known of the bullion coins are the American Gold Eagle and the South African Krugerrand. Several other countries produce bullion coins each year, including Australia, Mexico, and the United Kingdom. While these coins are stamped with some sort of face value, the value of the gold of which they are composed is typically far higher.

Bullion coins make for a great investment as they are small and easily transported. Most people will be comfortable using them as currency, should the need arise. As they are minted by governments, you can be reasonably certain of their purity as well. I would caution you, though, that if you desire to pursue acquiring bullion coins, you do so via a reputable dealer.

Gold can also be purchased in bar form. However, as noted earlier, these tend to be quite heavy and, as a result, may be difficult to transport or use in any practical sense. Gold bars will be stamped with their purity by the manufacturer. "Three nines" is a common phrase, referring to a bar that is 99.9 percent pure. In addition to being very heavy, gold bars are, of course, rather expensive.

SILVER

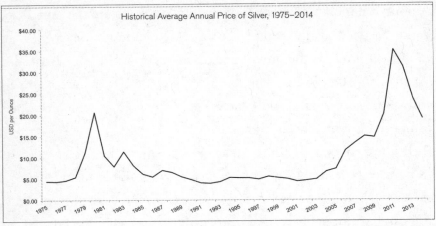

Historical Average Annual Price of Silver, 1975–2014

source: www.silverinstitute.org

Similar to gold, silver saw a dramatic spike in value during the Great Recession but has since started to return to more sane levels.

Silver is another interesting element and its use as currency is well-known throughout history. In addition to being the most reflective metal on the planet, it is one of the best conductors of electricity. It doesn't rust and is soft enough to mold and shape relatively easily. Silver is also the best thermal conductor among all metals.

Among precious metals, silver is unique in that it appears to have some medicinal properties as well. While studies are inconclusive as to the positive effects it has on infections and such, silver is an efficient antibacterial and antifungal. This has led to its use in socks and other garments as a means to control odor.

By and large, though, silver is mostly known for being second only to gold as an investment in precious metals.

For those looking to purchase silver for investment purposes, it is available in several forms. It has long been used to create beautiful and functional objects, such as silverware and jewelry. Silver is also available as coins and bullion.

STERLING SILVER

Pure silver is generally not used for things like art, jewelry, or silverware. That's typically reserved for sterling silver, an alloy consisting of 92.5 percent silver and 7.5 percent copper. Like gold, silver is a soft metal, so the addition of copper hardens it and makes it more durable.

Sterling silver objects are usually stamped with the number 925, indicating the 92.5 percent pure silver. Other stamps include 900 and 800, meaning 90 percent or 80 percent silver content, respectively.

If you are unsure whether an item is truly silver rather than just being silver-plated (and a jeweler isn't available to assess the item), there are a few tests you can perform.

Silver is only slightly magnetic. If you use a strong magnet (a rare earth one made of neodymium is best), there should only be a faint attraction to the item. If the item you are testing is flat, such as a bar, hold it at an angle and let the magnet slide down its side. A positive indication for silver would be the magnet very slowly sliding, not sticking in one place or shooting down the slope like a downhill skier.

Because of the high thermal conductivity of silver, you can use ice to test for silver content. This experiment is actually kind of cool, no pun intended. It doesn't work well on jewelry but is great for coins and bars. Take an ice cube and place it on the object to be tested. The ice should immediately begin to melt, as though you'd placed it on a hot pan.

Many of us preppers have bleach on hand for water purification purposes. You can also use a drop of bleach to test for silver content. Silver tarnishes very quickly in the presence of bleach. Simply put one drop of bleach on the item being tested. If it turns black right away at the point of contact, it is likely silver. Note, however, that this test should be done in conjunction with one of the others, as even silver-plated items will react in this fashion.

SILVER COINS

Silver had been used for coinage long before Judas received his thirty pieces. The Greeks were among the first to mass-produce silver coins, called *drachmas*. Since that time, most cultures have used silver in their coins.

Given that silver, while precious, isn't nearly as valuable as gold, it has been used even in modern times as a convenient material for currency. The American Silver Eagle and the Canadian Silver Maple Leaf are two of the more commonly found silver coins still produced today. Others include the Chinese Silver Panda and the Australian Silver Kangaroo.

Then we have what is commonly referred to as "junk silver." Up until 1965, American coins had an appreciable amount of real silver in them. Odds are pretty good that if you have a coin jug at home, you'll probably find at least a few of these coins among the rest. The following United States coins are all 90 percent silver:

Roosevelt dimes (1946–1964)

Mercury dimes (1916–1945)

Washington quarters (1932–1964)

Franklin half-dollars (1948–1963)

Kennedy half-dollars (1964)

There are others as well, such as the Liberty Head quarters and dimes produced through 1916, but these are far rarer than the ones noted above. I suggest you set up two coin jars. At the end of each day, dump out all your loose change and glance through it. Place any junk silver coins into one jar and the rest into the other.

SILVER ROUNDS

Silver rounds are basically privately minted coins of one sort or another. They cannot be recognized as actual currency as they were not minted by the government. Rounds are created as gifts or souvenirs for individuals or companies, typically to commemorate some sort of event. They will not have any sort of face value stamped on them, again, because they aren't true coins. They will, however, generally have the weight (often 1 troy ounce) and the purity of the silver marked on the round.

SILVER BARS

While silver bars are certainly available, I do not recommend them as an investment. As with gold bars, you'll have a hard time transporting or using them in any sort of practical sense.

ALTERNATIVE PRECIOUS METALS

While gold and silver are the first precious metals that usually come to mind when we talk about investments, there are others to consider.

THE PLATINUM GROUP

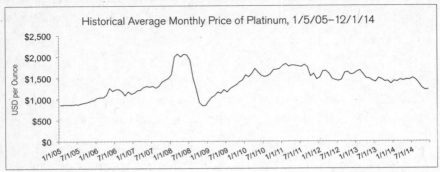

Historical Average Monthly Price of Platinum, 1/5/05–12/1/14

source: www.platinum.matthey.com

Unlike gold and silver, platinum values dropped in 2008 along with the economy. They rebounded decently between 2009–2011 but have eased downward ever since.

The platinum group consists of six metals that are similar to one another on a chemical or elemental level. They are:

Platinum

Iridium

Palladium

Rhodium

Osmium

Ruthenium

These metals are very dense and durable and have use in both jewelry and manufacturing. Much of the world's supply comes from mines in South Africa. Of the six, two are generally available for investment, at least in terms of being able to purchase and hold physical coins—platinum and palladium.

The United States Mint, back in 1997, began producing Platinum American Eagle bullion coins. These have a face value of $100, though that is largely symbolic. The coin contains 1 ounce of platinum.

Below are three economic charts. In the first chart, we see the daily trading rates of platinum over the last ten years. Below that are the mean monthly rates (each month's daily rates averaged over the same period), and the final chart shows the annual mean trading rates for each year.

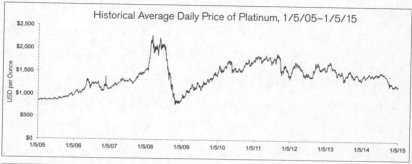

Historical Average Daily Price of Platinum, 1/5/05–1/5/15

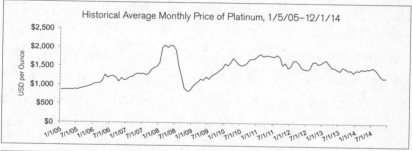

Historical Average Monthly Price of Platinum, 1/5/05–12/1/14

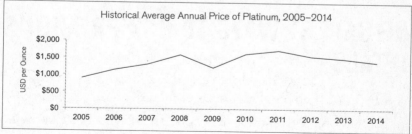

Historical Average Annual Price of Platinum, 2005–2014

source: www.platinum.matthey.com

All three charts are made up of the same data but tell very different stories. The day trader is going to see a lot of everyday volatility in the market, but the long-term investor can count on a relatively stable investment when it comes to precious metals.

Canada joined the club in 2009, offering a Platinum Maple Leaf coin containing 1 troy ounce. It was first issued back in 1988 and was minted until 2002. During this run, there were actually several coins issued, with varying denominations. However, the value of platinum began fluctuating wildly and the Canadian government discontinued minting the coins until 2009, this time with only one face value and design.

As for palladium coins, the two primary options are the Palladium Maple Leaf from Canada and the Palladium Panda from China.

Platinum group metals suffer the same problems, though, as other precious metals in that you may find it difficult to trade them with someone who doesn't know their value or has no way to independently verify their authenticity. Minted coins will likely be seen as legit to a layperson, who may balk at platinum or palladium in favor of gold or silver.

There is, however, some investment value here. A savvy trader could purchase platinum when the price is low and trade it at a profit later when the price is high. In doing so, he or she could stand to gain a substantial profit, though obviously there are risks to such a plan.

THE SAFEST WAYS TO BUY PRECIOUS METALS

If you are looking to purchase precious metals, there are a few options out there among a whole lot of scams. Those who don't know how to determine the value and authenticity of the metal are at a great disadvantage and can be easy prey for the charlatans.

One of the first places many turn to is the Internet. In recent years, there has been a huge surge in websites offering to buy and sell precious metals. The problem is, how do you know which ones are trustworthy? The simple answer to that is, you don't. It is for that reason alone that I would encourage you to find a local dealer, a company you can visit in person to make your purchases.

An excellent resource is the Professional Numismatists Guild (www.pngdealers.org). They are a nonprofit organization consisting of coin and precious metal dealers who adhere to a strict code of ethics. On their website, they offer a searchable database of dealers. With a little digging, you should be able to locate a reputable dealer in your local area. While numismatists are known primarily for coins, most dealers will happily assist you in procuring bullion and such.

Another option, provided you know what you're doing, is to visit pawnshops. Some are quite nice, others, well, not so much. The decent ones will have staff on hand or who are available on short notice to assist you with choosing gold and silver jewelry that will meet your needs. Always ask about the return policy on the items you are purchasing. Furthermore, don't just accept their word when it comes to determining the actual worth of what you've purchased. Take the necklace or ring to a jeweler and have it appraised. If the pawnshop led you astray and sold you a gold-plated bracelet that was purported to be solid gold, take the appraisal with you to prove your case and ask for a refund.

While you're at the jeweler getting your item appraised, see what they have to offer. It wouldn't hurt to ask them about purchasing damaged or broken jewelry, given that you just want it for the precious metal content.

In just about every moderately sized city in America, you'll find at least one "Cash for Gold" sort of business. They've been cropping up everywhere in the last few years. I would caution you strongly about doing business with many of them. In my experience, the majority are relatively new and lack any sort of reputation, good or bad. They tend to cater to those who are in desperate need of immediate cash and, as a result, can often be seen as predatory, whether or not that's actually the case.

DIAMONDS AND GEMSTONES

Precious gems are yet one more possibility as a hedge against the future. While I'll talk a bit about diamonds, rubies, and other sparkly goodies, I tend to shy away from recommending them wholeheartedly as investments. The average person lacks the specialized knowledge and equipment to adequately test for counterfeits and lookalikes. I mean, it's one thing to buy a diamond bracelet from a reputable dealer, complete with the requisite paperwork certifying authenticity, and selling it to another jeweler later. Quite another thing to be presented with a purported diamond and ruby necklace and asked to accept it as payment for a box of ammunition.

As with anything else, buyer beware. Keep any and all paperwork associated to purchased gemstones. Should you need to unload any of it in a hurry, those documents may go far in expediting the process.

DIAMONDS

As many of us know, diamonds, as well as all colored gemstones, are rated or classified based on the "Four Cs": cut, clarity, color, and carat weight. A diamond is cut in certain ways that allow it to reflect the maximum amount of light. The better the cut, the greater the sparkle. The clarity refers the amount of imperfections within the stone. The clearer the stone, the greater the clarity. Color is, well, the color of the stone. Colorless is the ideal. Carat weight is the total mass of the stone. In other words, the actual size. Be aware of the term "total carat weight," too. If you have an object that has multiple stones, the TCW (total carat weight) refers to the total of all stones present.

Of the Four Cs, the cut is generally seen as the most important for determining the beauty of the diamond. In the diamond world, size is important but takes a backseat to beauty.

EMERALDS

If cut is the most important component with diamonds, color ranks the highest with emeralds and other gemstones. Emeralds are green, of course, and the greener the better. Clarity is also important, as well.

Where diamonds are typically examined through a loupe, which is a simple eyepiece that provides ten-times magnification, emeralds are simply looked at without an aid. If the stone has no imperfections noticeable to the naked eye, it is considered "eye clean." Because emeralds tend to have numerous surface fissures, they are often oiled prior to being sold. Cedar oil or another similar oil is used to fill in cracks and such on the surface of the stone. This is considered a routine practice in the gem world.

SAPPHIRES

Sapphires are generally thought of as being blue, but there are other colors out there, including yellow and green. The so-called "star sapphire" is a special type, where cracks beneath the surface intersect and, as a result, a six-sided "star" shines from within the stone when light is refracted through it. There is also what is called a "pink sapphire," which is actually a ruby.

Sapphires are often heat-treated to enhance their color. Sometimes an impurity, such as beryllium, is intentionally diffused into the gem during the heat treatment, leading to further improvement of the natural color.

RUBIES

Rubies form the red component of our gemstone rainbow. The most valuable rubies are a deep, blood-red color. Rubies are the third hardest of the natural gemstones, trailing diamonds and moissanites. Like other gemstones, natural rubies almost always have imperfections called rutile needles, commonly called silk. It is the presence of this silk within the stone that allows gemologists and others to determine whether the stone is natural or manmade.

Rubies, like sapphires, are often heat-treated to enhance the color. If this has been done, it should be noted on the paperwork accompanying the gems.

Gemstones are typically sold as part of an item of jewelry, rather than as loose stones. As a result, the overall value has to take into account all of the stones as well as the gold or silver used to create the bracelet, ring, or necklace. This does add a possible complication to the use of these items of jewelry for investment or purchasing power in the event of an economic collapse. Where it is fairly easy to cut a gold or silver coin into pieces, should the need arise, breaking a necklace or bracelet tends to devalue the whole works.

If I had my druthers, I'd find precious metals, particularly coins and rounds, far more preferable to gemstones when it comes to investment in these sorts of material goods.

THE SAFEST WAYS TO PURCHASE GEMSTONES

As with buying precious metals, if you aren't experienced with grading gemstones yourself, you'll need to find those with the knowledge and background. By far, your best bet will be to speak with a local, reputable jeweler. Explain to him or her that you're looking to invest in precious stones and see what they have to offer.

An honest jeweler will happily provide a certificate of authenticity as well as information related to the provenance of the stones. This means they'll gladly tell you where they got them, and it probably won't be some weird story about a little old man and falling into the deal of a lifetime.

Fake gems can be nearly impossible to discern from the real deal without specialized equipment and training. If you lack either of them, stick with buying from local dealers with strong reputations for honesty and integrity.

CHAPTER 5

POST-COLLAPSE BARTER AND TRADE GOODS

What to stockpile for future use in bartering is a popular topic on the various survival and prepper online forums. Some of the items often suggested, such as tobacco or matches, may be deemed common sense. Others, though, such as prescription medications, seem logical but in the real world prove problematic, whether it is in their acquisition or storage. When it comes to deciding what to set aside for possible post-collapse bartering, here are a few rules.

FIRST, THE ITEMS MUST HAVE INHERENT VALUE TO YOU. Remember, there's a possibility you'll never have the opportunity to use the items for barter. The idea here is to choose a few things you'd normally use anyway and stock up on extra for trading purposes, should the need arise.

NEXT, THE ITEMS MUST BE FAIRLY SHELF-STABLE. The last thing you want is to spend time, energy, and funds amassing quantities of barter goods, only to have them deteriorate or otherwise go bad before you get the chance to use them in a trade.

FINALLY, THE ITEMS MUST BE RELATIVELY INEXPENSIVE NOW. I realize "inexpensive" is a relative term. What is cheap to me might be costly to another. However, what you want to avoid is spending a ton of money purchasing items that you plan to designate as barter goods. It makes little sense to sink thousands of dollars into your version of wampum with the result being you can't afford basic necessities for your own family.

SUGGESTED BARTER GOODS

So, what are some items that meet those requirements? Let's group the items into categories.

VICES

Likely, the most desirable items for trading in the immediate aftermath of a collapse will be the sorts of things that aren't good for us but that we're accustomed to having on a regular basis. **Tobacco** is high on the list because smokers will probably trade almost anything to get their nicotine fix. Now, before I get all sorts of nasty letters and emails, yes, I fully realize that tobacco probably violates one or two of those rules we just talked about. If you're not a smoker, you have no inherent use for it. Plus, it isn't all that cheap nowadays. However, every rule has an exception and I feel the barter value of tobacco is high enough to justify its inclusion here.

As an alternative to cigarettes, pick up a few canisters of loose tobacco and boxes of rolling papers (or cheap pipes) to lessen the impact on your budget. Smokers who are deep in the throes of a nicotine fit will gladly roll their own. Wrap the canisters in foil and keep them in your freezer. The tobacco won't stay fresh forever, but I doubt many smokers will chafe at a stale flavor.

Next up on the list of vices is **alcohol**. Even those who aren't die-hard alcoholics may be interested in a little something to take the edge off. Beer, unless you're making your own as you go along, won't last very long on the shelf. Distilled spirits, though, have an indefinite shelf life, as long as they remain unopened. Now, I'm not talking about fancy liqueurs like Bailey's Irish Cream. I'm referring to the base liquors such as tequila, vodka, whiskey, rum, and brandy. If you decide to add some booze to your barter stockpile, I suggest going with the half-pint (200 ml) or the pint (375 ml) bottles, rather than the fifth (750 ml) or larger sizes. When you are bartering, the other person may indeed have something you desire, but it might not be valuable enough to warrant a large bottle of whiskey.

In keeping with our "inexpensive" rule, there's no need to stockpile bottles of Glenfiddich. A few bottles of any no-name popskull will be quite fine.

For the caffeine addicts, **coffee** and **tea** will be highly prized. While I'm sure many coffee connoisseurs would turn their noses at it now, instant will likely not be turned down. Green (unroasted) coffee beans can be roasted at home as well, if you're opting for something of higher quality. Green coffee beans will stay reasonably fresh for two or three years, while roasted beans should be used within days to a few weeks at the most. Instant coffee will remain good for a year, perhaps a bit less, if unopened. Once the jar is unsealed, though, only a few weeks.

Generally speaking, loose tea will be good for a couple of years and tea bags for about eighteen months, assuming proper storage. Once the packages have been opened, the tea begins to lose flavor rather quickly. While it won't go "bad" and pose a health risk, tea made with older bags or loose tea leaves won't taste very good.

While we're on the subject, consider picking up a bottle or two of **caffeine tablets**. These aren't very expensive and will likely have great value to those who are suffering the effects of caffeine withdrawal. I can tell you from experience that the headaches are not a whole lot of fun.

Cocoa mix may also have great barter value. Plus, it is a welcome treat on a cold day. With a shelf life of only about seven to ten months, it isn't great for long-term storage, but if your family is anything like mine, they'll be happy to help you rotate the supply regularly.

I would also include **candy** on our list of vices. Chocolate bars don't tend to last long on the shelf, but hard candies do just fine, provided you keep them cool and away from high humidity. Spending just a few bucks at your local dollar store on some bags of peppermints or butterscotch could prove to be a wise investment.

VICES LIST

- ❑ Alcohol
- ❑ Caffeine tablets
- ❑ Candy
- ❑ Cocoa mix
- ❑ Coffee
- ❑ Tea
- ❑ Tobacco, rolling papers, pipes

CONSUMABLES

If there's one good thing that might come out of a collapse, it may be that you will no longer have to hide homegrown zucchini in your neighbor's mailbox in an effort to get rid of some of it. Instead, you might trade it for some apples from their tree or perhaps a few eggs. Excess **garden produce** will probably fetch a good price on the barter market. If you have a root cellar or other means of food preservation (and you certainly should have one or both of those covered), you could even provide veggies and fruit in the off season, increasing their market value substantially.

The foresight to stock up on **heirloom seeds** may prove to be rather profitable. For the uninitiated, heirloom seeds are true strain varieties, meaning the seeds collected from the vegetables may be planted and grown. Kept cool, dry, and in a dark place, seeds will remain viable for quite some time. I suggest purchasing packets of heirloom seeds and storing them away without opening the packets. This way, you'll be in a much better position to verify the seed types and assure potential traders that they are indeed heirloom varieties. Otherwise, you could just as well tell people you have Jack's magic beans for all the proof you'll be able to provide.

Stock up on extra **baking staples**. There will no doubt be something of a learning curve for many people when it comes to baking bread and other goodies. When running to the grocery store for a new loaf or some rolls isn't a feasible option any longer, you could be in a position to trade them some of the basic ingredients.

Sweeteners, such as honey or sugar, last almost forever and will be highly prized. Honey in particular also has many health benefits.

There are good reasons why **beans** and **rice** are considered staple foods for preppers. They are cheap, easy to prepare, and filling. Adding a few extra sacks of each to your storage could give you some buying power later.

To help offset nutritional deficiencies, some folks may seek **multivitamins**. Even if they aren't actively searching for them, they

DID YOU KNOW?

Throughout history, salt has been an important commodity. In fact, the word *salary* stems from the Latin word *salarium*, which was a Roman soldier's payment made in salt.

may show interest in the availability of a bottle. If you decide to stock up on a few extra bottles, find those with the most distant expiration dates you can. Multivitamins don't go "bad," but they begin to lose potency at some point after the expiration date. As with most other things you store, keep them cool and out of the light.

The right **spices** and **herbs** can make or break a meal. However, most spices are best when fresh. But, if you can store them in airtight containers out of direct light, they'll last longer. What you might consider doing is adding common herbs to your garden and drying them after harvesting. While technically neither an herb nor a spice, *garlic* can be rather prolific, is enjoyed by many people, and has great health benefits to boot.

While it is a mineral, **salt** often falls into the spice category. It is incredibly cheap and lasts nearly forever. Salt has many uses, including flavoring food, alleviating a sore throat when gargled with, preserving food, and acting as a cleaning agent.

CONSUMABLES LIST

- ❑ Baking staples (flour, sugar, etc.)
- ❑ Beans
- ❑ Garden produce
- ❑ Heirloom seeds
- ❑ Multivitamins
- ❑ Rice
- ❑ Salt
- ❑ Spice, herbs
- ❑ Sweeteners

MEDICAL SUPPLIES

Easy access to medical care is sure to disappear after a collapse. Add to that the inability to run to the store for cough medicine and you'll have people scrambling for a slew of different medical supplies. **Pain relievers** and **fever reducers** like acetaminophen and ibuprofen will be high on that list. Both are fairly inexpensive, with shelf lives of about five years from the date of manufacture.

Other common over-the-counter medications that may be in demand include **antacids**, **anti-diarrheals**, **antihistamines**, **cold remedies**, and **cough syrup**. Along these same lines, **burn cream**, **antibiotic ointment**, and **analgesic ointment** will likely have some trade value.

Various first aid supplies will be of interest to most people as well, such as adhesive bandages, **moleskin dressing**, **latex or nitrile gloves**, **gauze pads**, and **elastic wraps**.

While I would never advocate anything illegal, nor will I suggest you deliberately skip doses in order to build up a supply, certain **prescription medications** will be of great value. Anything narcotic will be prized, as will antibiotics. Be careful of their shelf lives, of course. I only mention this category of trade goods because there may well be family members who don't survive the initial days of a collapse, sad to say, and small supplies of these medications may then be available.

A subcategory here that is very important to consider is **feminine health**. Many women maintain a supply of menstrual pads and/or tampons to last perhaps one or two of their cycles. That being the case, these items will command a good price on the barter market. Yeast infection creams and medications for treating similar conditions will also be highly valued. Even if you don't have females in your household, you might consider picking up some of these items, or at least asking a female friend to do so for you.

- ❑ Analgesic ointment
- ❑ Antacids
- ❑ Antibiotic ointment
- ❑ Anti-diarrheals
- ❑ Antihistamines
- ❑ Burn cream
- ❑ Cold remedies
- ❑ Cough syrup
- ❑ Elastic wraps
- ❑ Feminine health products (menstrual pads, yeast infection creams, etc.)
- ❑ Gauze pads
- ❑ Gloves (latex or nitrile)
- ❑ Moleskin dressing
- ❑ Pain relievers, fever reducers (acetaminophen, ibuprofen)
- ❑ Prescription medications

HAND TOOLS

There are two approaches you might consider when it comes to tools as trade goods. The first and likely better option if the trade is being made with people in your neighborhood is to offer the use of the tool(s) for a rental fee of sorts. Failing that, a permanent trade could be arranged. Hand tools, such as **hammers, saws, wrenches, screwdrivers,** and **pliers** will all be in demand.

Any of the tools commonly used for clearing brush and procuring firewood will also have great value—**axes, hatchets, bow saws, machetes,** and the **accessories necessary for sharpening them.** In keeping with our rule about expenses, I suggest haunting flea markets and rummage sales, picking up extra tools only when you find good quality at a cheap price.

Knives are among the most useful tools, both now and after a collapse. However, as with hand tools, there are inexpensive knives and there are flat-out cheap ones. Avoid the latter if at all possible. If the blade is stamped "China" or "Pakistan," drop it and move on, no matter how small the price tag. Granted, there are some blades produced in China that are very well made. But the vast majority of them are more for the collectible market and not suited for our needs here. While a cheap knife may be better than no knife at all, trading crap may lead to people not wanting to deal with you anymore.

Some preppers suggest investing in spare **generators** or **solar panels** to use for barter. These are generally too pricey to buy extras, and I wonder what someone else could offer in trade to justify the expense. An alternative, though, may be to provide the power to charge batteries or devices, keeping the generator or solar panels to yourself.

Tarps and **cordage** may be relatively common in many garages, but I could easily see the need for extras. **Paracord**, due to its strength, is well-known among preppers as the cordage of choice for many tasks.

Batteries are another commonly suggested barter item. I'm on the fence about that, personally. On the one hand, I'm sure they would have value to many people. However, they aren't cheap, and rechargeable batteries are even more expensive than regular ones. If you decide to stock up on extra batteries for trading, you might want to pick up a battery tester as well so you can show people the remaining charge.

HAND TOOLS

- ❏ Axes
- ❏ Batteries
- ❏ Cordage
- ❏ Generators, solar panels
- ❏ Hammers
- ❏ Hatchets
- ❏ Knives
- ❏ Machetes
- ❏ Paracord
- ❏ Pliers
- ❏ Saws
- ❏ Screwdrivers
- ❏ Sharpening tools
- ❏ Tarps
- ❏ Wrenches

HYGIENE SUPPLIES

Maintaining at least some semblance of hygiene is not only healthy but helps people feel human. Long, hot showers may be nonexistent after a collapse. Lukewarm sponge baths may be the best many people can do. With that in mind, **soap** and **shampoo** are great barter items. Any time you happen to stay at a hotel, grab and save all you can. Ask around to family and friends about this as well. Someone my wife knows used to travel extensively for work and had accumulated a few shoeboxes full of this stuff.

While maintaining a smooth face for men or legs for women may not be a priority, the very luxury of it may be worth setting aside some **razors**. See, here's the thing. If you've ever experienced being on the wrong side of a failing budget, you know all too well how the little things can really brighten your day. Finding an extra $10 and treating yourself and your spouse to takeout pizza can feel pretty damn good. After a collapse, people will want and need what seem like the most

BARTERING FOR FUTURE PROFIT

While silver candlesticks and antique oil paintings have little to no actual survival value, don't overlook the possibility of accepting a few items like that and stashing them away for later. Odds are almost 100 percent that at some point down the road, order will be reestablished and things will return to some semblance of normalcy. After that occurs, the shiny doodads you collected may turn out to be worth a tidy sum.

I'm not suggesting you risk your family going hungry for the sake of taking in a Monet that was liberated from a local museum. But if the opportunity of taking possession of a something that is likely to be rather valuable in the future presents itself, without undue risk to yourself or your family, it is worth considering.

trivial things to bring a bit of sunshine into their lives. Scraping away several weeks of facial hair could be just the thing.

Of course, no discussion on hygiene would be complete without mentioning **toilet paper**. I'd be willing to bet even a single roll of the stuff will be worth quite a lot.

Dental floss, **toothbrushes**, and **toothpaste** will all be important for dental health. All are inexpensive and last a long time on the shelf.

HYGIENE SUPPLIES

- ❑ Baby wipes
- ❑ Dental floss
- ❑ Deodorant
- ❑ Diapers
- ❑ Razors
- ❑ Shampoo
- ❑ Soap
- ❑ Toilet paper
- ❑ Toothbrushes
- ❑ Toothpaste

CLOTHING

Most people likely have enough shirts, pants, and sweaters to get by without needing to buy more any time soon. But being able to offer a new pair of **socks** as a trade item might be enough to seal a deal. They aren't expensive and are pretty much one size fits all. Some folks also suggest packs of new **underwear**, but there is such a range of sizes, you'd have to be pretty lucky to happen to have some that will fit a random barter customer.

One would be wrong to assume that folks living in colder climates already have a good supply of **knit hats**, **scarves**, **gloves**, and **mittens**. There are many people, particularly those who live in urban areas, who own the bare minimum of these sorts of things. They've grown accustomed to living and working in temperature-controlled buildings, braving the elements only during brief runs to and from vehicles.

Given the expected lack of shopping opportunities, being able to offer up **needles**, **thread**, or **patches** may be quite handy. So-called **Shoe Goo** may also prove useful.

CLOTHING AND CLOTHING REPAIR

- ❑ Gloves, mittens
- ❑ Knit hats
- ❑ Needles
- ❑ Patches
- ❑ Scarves
- ❑ Shoe Goo
- ❑ Socks
- ❑ Thread
- ❑ Underwear

MISCELLANEOUS BARTERING ITEMS

Of course, a ton of items don't fall neatly into any one category and some of them may be just the ticket for your barter stash.

Anything to do with making fire, such as **matches**, **butane lighters**, and **ferro rods** will be vital for all collapse survivors. Yes, there are several primitive ways of making fire and learning how to use a bow drill or fire plough should be on any prepper's to-do list. Odds are pretty good the average person will need some help with getting a cooking fire going.

Candles are also very cheap, particularly if you hit some of the clearance sales after Christmas. If you can keep them in a cool corner of the basement, they'll last a long time and be ready when you want to offer them for trade.

Something few people think about until they need them themselves is **reading glasses**. You can find them for just a few bucks at any drug store. I suggest picking up a few in different strengths.

Magnifying glasses may also be of use to people and again are fairly cheap if you shop around.

As stored food grows scarce, **fishing supplies** may become highly prized. Spending just a few bucks can net you a good supply of extra hooks, line, bobbers, and other basic gear.

In the weeks following the initial collapse, many people will begin to realize that they need to learn new ways of doing things, and quite often, those "new" ways are actually how things were done in decades past. Having access to **how-to manuals** may prove to be rather lucrative for you. Topics covered by these books could include gardening, various types of home repair, trades (plumbing, electrical, etc.), food preservation, and even butchering.

Heavy-duty garbage bags have many uses, from expedient rain ponchos to bags for household waste. This item in particular is one few people may already have in great quantity in their home. Once they realize the need, you'll be able to provide. Smaller **plastic bags**, particularly those that have a zipper-lock closure, may also be in need.

Various types of entertainment items, such as **board games, paperback books, playing cards, dice**, and **puzzle books** (crossword, find-a-word, Sudoku, etc.) will certainly come in handy if the Internet, cable TV, and media players aren't functioning due to a lack of electricity or some other reason. All of these things can be found for pennies at rummage sales and thrift stores.

As people begin to learn, or relearn, food preservation techniques such as home canning, they will quickly realize they need the requisite supplies, particularly **canning lids**. Picking up a few cases of these when you find them at a good price will be of benefit to yourself as well as those with whom you may be trading in the future.

Simple items for general purpose cleaning, such as **vinegar** and **baking soda**, will be highly valued among those who run out. **Bleach** can be used for water purification as well, though the shelf life is only about six months after it has been opened.

One last miscellaneous item to consider—**condoms**. With a distinct lack in television viewing as well as no Angry Birds to play with, many people may decide to resort to more...old-fashioned... means of entertainment. Not only do condoms work well for their intended purpose, they can also be used for portable water storage and keeping rifle barrels dry in the rain.

MISCELLANEOUS

- ❑ Art supplies
- ❑ Baking soda
- ❑ Bleach
- ❑ Board games
- ❑ Books (paperbacks, puzzle books)
- ❑ Candles
- ❑ Canning lids
- ❑ Condoms
- ❑ Dice
- ❑ Fishing supplies (hooks, line)
- ❑ Heavy-duty garbage bags
- ❑ How-to manuals
- ❑ Magnifying glasses
- ❑ Matches, butane lighters, ferro rods
- ❑ Notebooks
- ❑ Pens, pencils
- ❑ Plastic bags (zipper-lock closure)
- ❑ Playing cards
- ❑ Reading glasses
- ❑ Strike anywhere matches
- ❑ Vinegar

Finally, there is a distinct drawback to relying upon barter goods as a means of commerce. With the exception of renewable resources like garden produce, once the items have been traded, they're gone. As we'll see in the next chapter, learning and refining certain skill sets can set you up with possible occupations in a post-collapse world. By providing a service to the community members, you can earn a decent, perhaps even lucrative, living.

CHAPTER 6

BARTERING SKILLS INSTEAD OF STUFF

Stockpiling barter items is all well and good, affording you the ability to make quick trades for things you may need, but once those items are gone, they're gone. Some of them, such as honey or garden produce, can theoretically be replenished, but most of them are finite. Once you've traded your last sewing needle, you're probably going to have a tough time getting any more of them.

Skills, on the other hand, don't diminish with use. In fact, the more you use them, the better they get, right? There are many skill sets that will translate quite well into what we can call *cottage industries* in the wake of an economic collapse. Many of them are also darn useful for your own personal benefit.

MEDICINE

Anyone who has experience in an area of medicine, from the paramedic all the way to the MD, will be highly prized within the community. Included in this category are dentists and those who are skilled in the use of natural medicine, such as herbal remedies. Of course, most of these skills aren't something you can just pick up on a whim but take years of schooling, training, and experience before proficiency is reached.

With people having more free time on their hands due to the absence of Facebook and Netflix, at some point in the not-too-distant future following a collapse, midwives might become rather popular.

VETERINARY MEDICINE

As time goes on after a collapse, more and more people will gradually return to what was once very common—raising animals for food. As a result, veterinarians will be needed to keep those critters healthy.

It is worth noting that many veterinary medicines, such as antibiotics, are the same as human medications, though sometimes in a different form, such as a powder as opposed to the tablet or pill. That being the case, a veterinarian's office could prove to be an excellent resource for pharmaceuticals after a collapse.

ANIMAL HUSBANDRY

Related at least tangentially to veterinary medicine, husbandry involves care and breeding of various animals, such as goats, chickens, pigs, and rabbits. Those who are brand new to raising food animals will need the guidance of the more experienced. Thinking outside the box for a moment, an arrangement might be made whereby another community member can provide you with animal feed in exchange for a rabbit or three every few months.

HOME BREWING

I've often said that if there is one person who will never go hungry after a collapse, it will be the one who can provide the hooch for the community. Whether it is wine, beer, mead, or booze, alcohol will always demand a market. Bear in mind, too, that this isn't just for consumption but for medicinal purposes as well.

SOAP MAKING

It might take some time for people to finally run down their supplies of Irish Spring, but when that happens, they'll be looking for someone to supply them with soap, shampoo, and other cleansers. Soap making isn't difficult, but there is a learning curve involved. Lye can be produced from wood ash and essential oils for scent can be procured from wild sources. Some of the best homemade soap uses goat's milk, so you might consider working out a trade agreement with someone in the community who can supply it.

Don't overlook learning how to make laundry detergent and other related products, too.

SEWING

Because running to the store to buy a new shirt to replace one that gets ripped won't be feasible after a collapse, those with the skills to repair clothing will find plenty of work, as will those with a fair hand knitting scarves, socks, and mittens. Innovation is something to keep in mind, too. Being able to take a pile of old rags and turn them into cloth diapers or menstrual pads will probably make you rather popular in the community.

Don't overlook the possibility of working with heavy materials like canvas and animal hide as well. Come the cold winter months, if you're the only person in town who can produce warm outerwear, you'll not go wanting for work.

HANDYMAN SKILLS

Anyone who is skilled with carpentry, plumbing, electrical, and other construction-type trades will probably be overwhelmed with work requests. People will need help with repairs as well as with building things like chicken coops and rabbit hutches as time goes on. This is an area where creativity and being able to think outside the box will be important. You'll have limited resources with which to work, so being able to adapt and make do will be of great benefit.

MECHANICS

Knowing how to repair and maintain engines and motors will go far in a world where people rely on generators and turbines to provide limited but necessary power. Having the background and expertise in how these things are supposed to operate will put you in a position where you can retrofit and improvise solutions if they aren't working properly.

COOKING

Sad to say, but many people today have not the first clue how to cook from scratch. If the food didn't come out of the freezer and slide from a box into the microwave, they're helpless. Scratch cooking isn't difficult, but it is time-consuming. If you are particularly skilled at taking odds and ends from the pantry and turning it all into a mouth-watering meal, you might be able to turn that skill into a way to keep both you and others fed.

While we're not necessarily talking about setting up any sort of restaurant here, that could be a possibility down the road at some point.

You might notice a running theme throughout this section. With several of these occupations, I've suggested ongoing barter agreements. They are a great way to pull the community together. They tend to foster a sense of togetherness, an "all for one and one for all" mentality that is crucial for the community to withstand and overcome the crisis.

BAKING

If you have access to the necessary supplies and skills, you'll likely fetch a high price for bread and other fresh-baked goods. There just aren't a whole lot of people today who know how to bake bread from scratch, particularly without the use of a standard oven, but almost everyone appreciates the final product.

Obviously, your standard gas or electric oven will likely be inoperable after a collapse, as will electric mixers and what not. Take the time now to learn how to build and use a brick oven, as well as hand-operated mixers. There is a learning curve here.

FOOD PRESERVATION

After a collapse, many people will put in gardens, some for the very first time in their lives. Assuming these gardens produce reasonably well, people will seek to preserve their harvest through the winter months and beyond. If you have experience with canning and dehydrating food, you could work out an arrangement where you take part of the harvest in exchange for processing all of it.

If you have a large root cellar, you might even be able to rent out space in it, exchanging that for a portion of what's being stored.

WOODCUTTING

In the absence of utilities, most people will burn firewood to provide heat as well as cook their food. If you have the right tools and skills, you could make a nice profit providing people with split wood, ready to burn. This is one area in particular where a lucrative arrangement could be made with others in the community. For example, you agree to provide the baker with firewood on a daily basis. In return, he or she pays you with two loaves of bread each day. You keep one loaf for you and your family, then trade the second one for other necessities.

With the right equipment and know-how, felled timber could also be turned into lumber to be used for building repairs.

TOOL SHARPENING

Tool and knife sharpening is a lost skill. There is an art to it and those who do it well will find profit in doing so for others. Sharp knives and tools are actually much safer to use than dull ones.

POWER GENERATION

With the right solar array and equipment, you could provide a service where you charge batteries and portable electronics. While MP3 players and the like are indeed luxuries, many people will gladly trade you a few goodies for the ability to keep listening to their favorite tunes.

AMMUNITION RELOADING AND GUNSMITHING

With enough supplies set aside, it is feasible to make a good living reloading ammunition for the hunters in the community. Many of those who are knowledgeable in reloading also have some skill with gunsmithing, which could prove lucrative. That said, this is one area where I'd caution you to take great care choosing a trade partner.

Giving ammunition to someone you don't know and trust could lead to trouble.

SECURITY

Anyone with law enforcement or military experience might be tapped to join the community's security force. While at first this might be on a volunteer basis, at some point those involved may work out a more formal arrangement. Bear in mind, too, that this doesn't just mean protecting the community from outside threats. As the community settles into a new routine, there will be rules or laws formulated that will need to be enforced. So, on top of what will be the equivalent of today's patrol officers, there will need to be some sort of judicial system in place.

WILD FOOD PROCUREMENT

Those who have exceptional skill with hunting, fishing, or trapping may find work providing food for the community as a whole. In some scenarios, I could easily see the creation of some sort of community kitchen, where citizens gather en masse for at least one meal a day. The supplies for this would come from those who are able to provide, perhaps for a larger share of the community bounty.

In this same vein would be gathering wild edible plants, herbs, and such.

TEACHING AND CHILD CARE

Despite what you'll hear from the children, schooling will always be necessary to one degree or another. Those who have experience teaching, whether in public schools, private schools, or private homes, will be in a position to step in.

In addition, parents of small children may seek someone they can trust to take care of the kids while they are working in the gardens or out hunting.

CANDLE MAKING

This fun hobby will have real value after a collapse. Perhaps an ongoing trade could be struck with a local beekeeper, where they'd give you beeswax in exchange for a steady supply of candles.

BLACKSMITHING

Another lost art with great potential down the road, blacksmithing isn't something you can enter into lightly. It takes a fair amount of investment in both materials and time to learn just the basics. Keep in mind, we're not really concentrating on horseshoes here but being able to either manufacture or repair tools and other necessities. This need not require the use of a giant forge, either. Many hobbyists do quite well with small, handmade forges made from old charcoal grills and other repurposed junk.

BUTCHERING AND TANNING

Even those hunters who reliably bring in game at almost every outing might not know how to properly dress and butcher their kills. One with these skills can make a decent living earning a small portion of the harvest.

Those who can add hide tanning to their butchering skills will be able to perhaps double their income by trading the finished pelts to those who can turn them into moccasins, gloves, and hats.

SCAVENGING

Some people out there just have a nose for scrounging. Whether it is a distributor cap or a pair of piano hinges, give them a day and they'll somehow come up with it. They seem to have either a photographic memory or some sort of telepathy to where they just know how to find what they seek. These folks will be of vital importance to the community. Give them a list of necessary items and a couple of security personnel for protection, and they'll come back with what is needed and more.

ENTERTAINING

I know this sounds frivolous but bear with me. Perhaps not in the days immediately following the collapse but later, after the community members settle into routines of one sort or another, they will welcome distractions from their no doubt work-filled, day-to-day existence. Concerts, skits, even comedy routines may be welcome. If you recall your history studies, you'll remember that during the Great Depression, people in large numbers sought distraction, even comfort, by visiting movie theaters.

SETTING YOUR PRICE

How will you decide what to charge for your products or services? This is, of course, very subjective. A lot depends upon what you need and what others have to offer. Remember, we're talking barter here, and all the screwdrivers in the world won't do you a bit of good if what you really need is a hammer. In many cases, you might not be able to have a set price, at least not until or unless the community creates some sort of widely accepted currency.

PAYMENT IN TRADE GOODS IS NOTHING NEW

Even in today's advanced and sophisticated society, trading goods for services happens all the time. I know an attorney who, over the years, has accepted a side of beef, golf clubs, rifles, even a car as payment for services rendered.

I'm not saying you should show up at the gas station and try to trade a tank of fuel for a few chickens, but in some circumstances, it might be worth your time to ask about bartering for what you need to have done.

Instead of set prices, each trade will have to be worked out individually, based largely upon what you need and what the other person can offer. For example, let's say you make a fair living using your treadle sewing machine to make and repair clothing. In the past, you've accepted a squirrel or a few eggs in exchange for darning a pair of socks and patching a pair of pants. Then, you somehow break the last needle for the sewing machine. All the eggs in town aren't going to get you back in business; if a guy showed up with a new needle for you, he could probably name his price.

It's important to be as fair and reasonable as possible with your pricing. People tend to have long memories with stuff like this and they will remember if you jacked them up for no reason other than greed. How you've treated people in the past may make the difference between that sewing machine needle costing you three pair of socks or half of your inventory.

FINDING WORK

For many professions, such as medical doctor, veterinarian, and dentist, many in the community will probably already know what you do and seek out your assistance when needed. Heck, you might already have a well-known home business selling homemade candles and soaps.

Otherwise, you'll have to rely upon word of mouth, since putting an ad in the newspaper probably won't be an option. Just let a few folks know your skills or products are available and they'll spread the word, especially if you do exceptional work at a fair price.

Sounds pretty much like how it works today, doesn't it?

STOCKING SUPPLIES

Many of these cottage industries require tools and supplies in order to provide the service or products. Should you plan to pursue one or another of these occupations after a collapse, you'd be wise to stock up now on everything you'll need to stay in business for a while. Preserving food, for example, will require an awful lot of canning jars and lids. You could make returning the jars part of the deal, but expect at least a small percentage of the jars to never turn up again.

On the other hand, as we've been saying all along, you can work on developing ongoing trade agreements with a few people. If that is an option you are considering, I strongly suggest you work on those relationships now, rather than waiting until after a collapse. When talking to folks about this sort of trade, you don't need to mention anything about planning for the future if you're not comfortable doing so. If, for example, you're pursuing making soap with goat's milk and you know of someone in the area who raises the animals, just ask them about trading some milk for a few bars of soap from time to time. Assuming the owner isn't making their own soap already, they'll probably be agreeable to the deal.

THE PSYCHOLOGY OF WORK

There is also something of a psychological component at work here. In today's society, most of us tend to identify ourselves by what we do for a living. Our self-worth stems from our occupation, at least to some degree. Often, our job also reflects how others see us, right or wrong. Think about it. When you meet someone new, what is usually the first question they have after learning your name? *So, what do you do for a living?* This is one reason why many women who transition from working outside the home to becoming stay-at-home mothers struggle with the decision. Because they don't see themselves as contributing to society by performing a job, one that is visible to others and recognized by their peers, they feel as though their worth is diminished. (In reality, this is far from being true. Taking the time to properly raise children is truly commendable and is, perhaps, one of the most important "occupations" on the planet.)

The point here is that by planning ahead for your role in a post-collapse community, you not only position yourself to earn a living of sorts but also give yourself the luxury of making the choice, rather than having that role assigned to you by fate, circumstance, or otherwise.

CHAPTER 7

SAFEGUARDING VALUABLES

All of the cash, coins, and precious metals in the world won't do you much good if someone takes them from you. Along with stocking up on valuables comes the need for keeping them safe. Sure, you could just stash your gold coins in the underwear drawer and rely upon your faith in humanity, but that probably won't end well for you.

The unfortunate reality is that there are bad people in the world who would take anything you have of value if given the slightest opportunity. Human beings, though, almost always make decisions based on risk versus reward. Plus, criminals want to act quickly. They want to get in, grab the goodies, and make their getaway as fast as possible. The longer they remain in your home, the more likely they are to be caught in the act. Because of these two principles—risk versus reward and a burglar's desire to act fast—the more you can do to delay them through the use of safes and other security options, the less likely you are to come home to an empty house.

WHY NOT BANKS?

In the event of a currency collapse or similar crisis, one of the first things that may happen is banks locking their doors. Even if you are a long-time customer, you're not going to be able to access your accounts, much less a safe deposit box. In fact, there is historical precedent where banks have seized all funds from account holders, leaving the customers high and dry.

I'm not suggesting you head to your bank, pull every dollar out, and bury it all in your backyard. That would make paying your bills a little interesting, to say the least. What I am saying, though, is to recognize the fact that banks are in control of all funds kept in them, no matter whose name is on the account. Being prepared is all about giving yourself options. Use your bank account for the basics, like paying bills and cashing checks. But keep at least some of your cash and valuables outside of those vaults, just in case.

SAFES

Like just about everything else in life, safes have good points and bad points. They are aces at keeping your stuff under lock and key, of course. Even a safe of moderate quality will foil the attempts of the average burglar. But many safes today, while strong, are also somewhat lighter than their counterparts from back in the day. This means a criminal need only load it into his trunk and take it home to work on at his leisure.

Good-quality safes aren't cheap, either. Sure, you could head down to your local discount retailer and buy a "fireproof" safe that fits under your bed for under $50. But, as I mentioned above, all Joey Safecracker needs to do is grab the safe itself and take it home to try drilling it open. Even if he doesn't succeed, do you think he's going to bring it back to you? Nope, whether he opens it or not, you're still out the valuables inside.

QUALITIES OF A GOOD SAFE

There are a few points to consider when it comes to purchasing a safe. These include the type, quality, and location. Safes comes in all sorts of shapes and sizes, allowing you to find just the right one for your situation, provided you're willing to shop around and consider the different options.

One of the first buzzwords you're likely to come across is *fireproof*. This is actually something of a misnomer as what they really mean is fire resistant. Usually, manufacturers or retailers will rate safes based upon the length of time the safe will protect the contents from heat, smoke, and possibly water damage. Many of the safes marketed as fire resistant, at least the ones where that is listed as the primary feature, are inadequate for keeping your valuables protected from thieves. These safes are often built using very thin metal that surrounds a thick layer of fire resistant material. This works well at keeping the contents safe from a fire but with just a hammer and chisel, a crook can gain access.

For securing precious metals and other valuables, you are far better off looking for a safe that is constructed of thick steel and has a robust lock. Sometimes, these heavier-duty safes are rated based upon the approximate value of the content they will protect. While this dollar figure is very subjective, the idea is to give some sort of ranking for the consumer to consider. A safe rated to protect $20,000 in contents is going to be of higher quality than one rated for $5,000.

As for location, wall safes are for the movies, not real life. The problem is they can be easily removed by sawing through the wall and studs. Often, they aren't all that robust, either, and rely solely upon being hidden. Which leads to the second problem with wall safes—burglars know where to look for them. They've seen all the same movies as the rest of us, after all. Another factor to consider with wall safes is that they typically offer little to no protection against fire.

Closets are another common location for safes. If the safe is properly anchored to the floor and strong enough to resist basic safe-cracking techniques, you should be fine. However, bear in mind that the hash marks on the safe's dial can be difficult to see in low light. You might end up needing a flashlight any time you want to open the safe.

Strong safes are heavy and therefore need to be placed where the floor will support the weight. For that reason, I'd suggest keeping the safe in a lower level of the home. Another consideration for location is convenience for you and your family. If the safe is placed in a dark, dank basement corner, you may end up finding all sorts of reasons why a given item doesn't really need to be placed into the safe. You want the safe to be someplace where you can easily access it with a minimum of inconvenience.

HIDING VALUABLES

A low-budget option for protecting your goodies is to hide them in your home. There are all sorts of places that burglars tend to overlook in their haste to find the good stuff and get out without being caught. However, there are also several hiding spots that seem like good ideas but in reality are among the first places criminals check.

WELL-KNOWN HIDING SPOTS

When Bobby Burglar enters a home, often the first stop is the master bedroom. We are creatures of habit and this is frequently where we tend to hide the good stuff. He'll check the closets for safes and jewelry boxes. He'll check under the bed and between the mattress and box spring, too. From there, he'll head into the bathroom and pilfer the medicine cabinet for any easy-to-sell drugs, such as narcotics. He'll also likely peek into the toilet tank as that's a very common place for folks to hide a few valuables, believe it or not.

In the kitchen, he'll check in the freezer and see if you're storing cold, hard cash next to your cold, hard frozen peas. Bobby will dump out every box of cereal on the shelf, too. And here you thought you were being sneaky with hiding your diamond tennis bracelet in that box of Cheerios.

Once upon a time, hiding valuables in a child's bedroom wasn't a bad idea. Given the propensity for crooks to concentrate their efforts on the master bedroom, people figured they wouldn't take much time to search a kid's bedroom, too. However, children today often have just as many high-end electronics, from laptops to flat-screen TVs, as do their parents, so burglars have learned to check there as well.

Burglars know all about those diversion safes, too. You know, the ones that look like cans of shaving cream and what not. They'll pick up likely looking possibilities and check the weight. If it seems off, they'll toss it into their loot bag for closer examination later.

Bobby Burglar will dump out all drawers and swipe a hand through all bookshelves, spilling everything onto the floor. He might upend all dirty laundry baskets as well. Look, he's already broken into your home and made a huge mess. Do you really think he's going to balk at pawing through your unmentionables?

So, knowing all of this, where within the home could we possibly hide our valuables to keep them safe? Well, we need to get a little creative, that's all.

RECOMMENDED HIDING PLACES

The fact that burglars want to get in and out as quickly as possible works to our advantage. They'll check the easy, well-known hiding spots and then move on.

Most of us have at least one place within the home, typically a basement or attic, where we store our junk. Clothes that have long since gone out of style and haven't fit us in years, sets of dishes that are missing a piece or three, mix tapes we made when we were in high school, that sort of stuff. We know we should just get rid of most of it but, well, out of sight, out of mind. I doubt anyone would notice yet one more box among all the others. Label it as "Grandpa's ties" or "Mom's old pajamas" and stash your goods inside. Consider putting a layer of old clothes over the top of your stuff before you tape the box shut, just in case someone peeks inside.

If your basement lacks a drop ceiling, you'll typically see one or more stretches of large-diameter PVC pipe running here and there. Adding another section of pipe is just a matter of a few bucks and perhaps an hour of work. Position the new run of PVC away from the existing runs as otherwise, it will look odd to even the most casual observer. Seal each end of your new pipe with threaded caps so you can easily access the contents.

All is not lost if your basement does have a drop ceiling. You could do the same PVC pipe trick, though it might take a little more work as you'll have to deal with all the hangers and whatnot that hold up the ceiling. You could also just pop up one of the ceiling tiles and install a few makeshift shelves between the joists. With the ceiling tile in place, few people would ever think to look there.

Paper currency and even some coins can be hidden inside picture frames throughout the house. Simply tape the currency to the inside of the frame backing. As long as the frames themselves don't appear valuable, I doubt many burglars are going to want pictures of your dog.

If you are somewhat handy, you could remove the kick plates that run along the bottom of your kitchen cabinets. There is usually empty space behind them, suitable for reasonably flat items or boxes. Use magnets or hook-and-loop patches to replace the kick plates. Another handyman special is to install fake electrical outlets. You can buy specially made ones that are fashioned into diversion safes. I know what I said earlier about criminals knowing to check for diversion safes. This is one that they likely won't take the time to seek out.

How about a few other, really off-the-wall suggestions?

Reasonably flat items could be placed into a sealed plastic bag and taped to the bottom of the cat litter box. Up to you whether you want to put it inside or outside the box.

Tape an envelope to the back of a file in your file cabinet, one that has absolutely nothing to do with anything financial.

If you have potted plants scattered throughout the house, you could stash a few coins or something of similar size in a plastic bag

LEAVING OUT BAIT

I know it sounds counterintuitive, but you might consider routinely leaving a small stack of currency out in the open, such as on a bedroom dresser. Not a ton of money, just a few twenties or a couple of fifties. Don't make it look obvious, either. Buy a birthday card at the dollar store and put the money in or near it. The idea is to give the crook something easy to snatch so they might spend less time searching for hidden valuables. Remember, they're in a hurry and want to get out of the house as quickly as possible, but they won't want to leave empty-handed. By giving them this bait money, they may be less inclined to turn your house upside down, giving you less mess to clean up later.

buried at the bottom of a pot. My wife is a plant fanatic and we have several very large houseplants. I'm telling you, we could probably stash a Buick in some of those pots.

When you're considering hiding places, keep in mind the frequency, or lack thereof, of how often you'll need to access the items you're hiding. You won't want to dig up a houseplant once a week just to add a few more things to your stash. On the other hand, that might be a great spot to put extra cash as you'll be less tempted to dig it out and spend it frivolously.

CACHES

Traditionally, caches are stashes of valuables or other goodies that are hidden outside the home. Those old mason jars Grandpa would fill with money and bury in the backyard? Yep, those are caches. These can be a great for protecting cash, precious metals, and such against theft and fire.

One of the most common DIY cache designs is to use a 4-inch-diameter PVC or ABS tube. For those unfamiliar, PVC is white and ABS is black. For our purposes, they are interchangeable so just get whichever fits into your budget better. While you're at the store, grab an end cap, an adapter with a cleanout plug, and either PVC cement or silicone caulk. When you get home, cut your tube to the desired length; probably a couple of feet will be sufficient, but go longer if you're planning on stashing a rifle or something of similar length. Put a bead of caulk or cement around one end of the tube and slide on the end cap. Do the same on the other end with the adapter. *Do not cement or caulk the actual plug, the piece with the threads that screws into the adapter.* Let the cement set for about twenty-four hours. Then, fill the tube with your goodies, toss in a couple of oxygen absorbers, and screw the plug on tight. The tube should now be watertight and ready for burying.

A twist on this concept is to build two tubes, one thin enough to fit inside the other. This is a great idea, assuming what you want to place into the cache will fit into the smaller-diameter tube. The reason this works well is because over time the ground settles and compacts. As a result, it can be very difficult to pull the outer tube from the soil. By placing one tube inside the other, the inner one will be easy to remove.

Now, where to hide the cache? It is best to bury the cache tube on property you own. This way, there are no issues regarding trespassing and such. Dig the hole deep enough that the top of the tube will be lower than the average frost line in your area of the country. If your area doesn't get that cold, shoot for 8–10 inches or so below the surface. Refill the hole with a few inches of soil, then scatter a few rusty bolts and screws around the area. This is to try and foil any seekers using metal detectors. Refill the hole completely and tamp it down. Scatter leaves and twigs over the newly turned soil to help camouflage it. It won't take too long before the spot is unrecognizable.

This, of course, leads to one last issue with caches. How do you find them again? How much would it suck to have hidden hundreds of dollars' worth of valuables and end up searching forever because you can't remember exactly where you buried it? There are a few ways to go about this. One of the most common is to use a triangulation approach. Locate three different, fairly immovable landmarks and position your cache between them, noting the distances from each landmark. My preferred method is to provide your own landmark. Find a rock that has an easy-to-recognize shape, something fairly flat and about the size of a dinner plate. Bonus points if it has a unique color to it as well. Position it not directly over your cache but a set distance to one side, say 2 feet to the left. Line it up with a large tree or other stationary object if you think that will help in locating your cache quickly and easily.

Keeping your valuables safe should be a high priority for you and your family. Take the time to come up with solutions, then stick with them. It can be entirely too easy to become complacent and figure, "It'll never happen to me." That thought process is exactly what leads to a high percentage of thefts.

CHAPTER 8

INVESTING IN SELF-SUFFICIENCY

Perhaps the single most important investment you can make toward a successful future is to become as self-sufficient as possible. The greater the number of your basic needs you can satisfy on your own, the less you will be impacted by some sort of societal breakdown. Think about it like this: Back during the Great Depression, the folks who saw the least amount of trouble were the ones out in the sticks who had been raising their own food all along.

As we go through a few of the categories of basic needs and illustrate what you can do to improve your self-sufficiency, please keep something in mind. Few people are in a position where they can do it all, at least right now. Don't let that inhibit you from taking at least a few steps in the right direction. Just because you don't have enough space in the backyard to start a massive 1,000-square-foot garden doesn't mean you can't grow at least *some* food for your family. Too many people give up before they've even started because they figure if they can't do it all, what's the point? Well, think of it as a building process. The Great Wall of China wasn't built in a single day...it started with a single brick.

FOOD PRODUCTION

Investing in the means to produce at least some amount of food for yourself and your family is an excellent way to dip your toe into the self-sufficiency pool. As I said earlier, you may not have the space or ability to grow edibles or raise animals for the majority of your meals, but don't let that stop you from getting started.

GARDENING

I firmly believe that no matter what your living arrangement is, you can grow *something* to feed your family. Even if it is only a couple of tomato plants and a barrel of potatoes, that's a start. If you've never grown anything other than dandelions before (which, by the way, make for great salad greens), now's the time to get moving. Make a list of the vegetables and fruits your family enjoys eating, then start doing some research on each of them. I mean, there's little sense in investing time and energy growing asparagus if no one in your family

WHAT IS HOMESTEADING?

As you explore various means of achieving a higher degree of self-sufficiency, you'll no doubt come across the term *homesteading*. In a general sense, homesteaders today are emulating, to one degree or another, the lifestyle of the pioneers who settled this country. They produce some or all of their own food, employ various means of preserving food, and basically strive to provide for most of their basic needs. In this modern age, homesteading also often includes producing power through solar panels, wind turbines, or other methods.

will touch it, right? There are a ton of resources available to help you get started. Talk to neighbors and friends who are more experienced than you. Ask them for advice on what plants grow best in your area and climate. Heck, if you ask nicely, they might even toss you some seeds.

Go online and seek out your local county extension office. They have Master Gardeners who will be more than happy to answer any questions you may have. Many of these offices offer classes throughout the year as well, either for free or for a nominal fee.

I would advise you to start small if this is your first garden. Food production, even as a hobby, is rather labor-intensive, and if you try to do too much at once, you may quickly become overwhelmed. You might be surprised at just how much food you can grow in one small garden bed.

If you are strapped for space, look into container gardening or square foot gardening. *Container gardening*, at its core, is simply growing plants in pots rather than in the ground. This is a great option for those who live in apartments or condos. While you won't be able to grow a ton of food on your patio, something is better than nothing. Another option for urban dwellers who lack yard space is to seek out *community gardens*. Arrangements are made with the owners of vacant lots where individuals or families are allowed space to plant small gardens. Each person is responsible for their own garden plot. These community gardens can be a great way to network with like-minded individuals as well as trade some of your excess produce.

Square foot gardening is another option for those with limited space. It is sort of a kissing cousin to container gardening in that all of your growing is limited to a defined area. Basically, you take your garden and divide it up in boxes, each one being, you guessed it, a square foot. Truth be told, you aren't actually making small boxes out of your garden but rather just using string to section off the space.

Each square is devoted to one or more plants, with each one planned in advance so as to complement its neighbors. For example, a crop that grows best in partial shade would be planted next to something that grows tall and thus blocks the sunshine a bit.

Don't overlook the possibility of adding a few fruit trees to the mix, either. While many varieties do require cross-pollination, you can grow apples or pears in a far smaller area than you might realize.

As you gain more experience with gardening, hopefully you'll be able to expand your plots each year, growing more and more of your own food. Not only will this positively impact your wallet, homegrown food is generally much healthier, not to mention tastier, than what you'll find at the grocery store.

WILD EDIBLES

Tasty, nutritious plants are all around us. Dandelion greens, for example, have a ton of calcium, vitamins A, E, and K, and iron. And here you thought it was just a bothersome weed! If you want to get a huge bang for your buck with regards to investing in self-sufficiency, learn to identify and prepare wild edibles. Pick up a guide to edible plants at the bookstore or library and get outside. A couple of guides I wholeheartedly endorse:

A Field Guide to Edible Wild Plants: Eastern and Central North America (Peterson Field Guides) by Lee Allen Peterson (1999, Houghton Mifflin Harcourt)

The Forager's Harvest: A Guide to Identifying, Harvesting, and Preparing Wild Edible Plants by Samuel Thayer (2006, The Forager's Harvest Press)

Concentrate on learning just a few local plants first. Learn to identify them in each stage of their development so if you run across

If you live in an area governed by some sort of HOA, I would strongly advise you to research the bylaws and guidelines to ensure you abide by any restrictions when it comes to planting a garden. Urban and suburban dwellers should do the same with municipal ordinances as well. It would be horrible to invest considerable time, energy, and expense in a garden, only to learn it needs to be removed immediately lest you incur fines.

Personally, I would never want to live in an area where growing a garden was verboten, let alone where others had a say in what color I painted my house or what kind of mailbox I wanted to put up. But, to each their own.

them but they're not quite ready for harvest, you can note the location and come back later. Gradually add them to your regular diet.

You should avoid harvesting wild edibles growing in areas that are treated with pesticides or that are subject to high amounts of pollution, such as on the side of a busy road. Also, be very wary of trespassing or harvesting plants in city-, county-, or state-owned areas.

MEAT PRODUCTION

This is an area that is slightly less accepted among neighbors than gardening. I mean, it's one thing to plant a few berry bushes along your back fence. Quite another to add a rabbit hutch and some free-range chickens to the mix. However, producing at least some of your own meat is a big step toward self-reliance.

Many municipalities have begun enacting ordinances that allow for raising backyard chickens, as well as a few other critters. A simple phone call to City Hall should let you know if you're in the clear to explore these options.

Both chickens and rabbits offer a great return on minimal investment. Chickens, of course, offer both meat and eggs, the latter of which could occasionally be gifted to neighbors to help offset any negative opinions on your new hobby. Other animals to consider include ducks, turkey, and goats. If you live a bit farther out from city limits, you might look into pigs as well.

As with gardening, when you're starting out with raising animals, you need to be careful not to overextend yourself. Even just a few chickens involves a lot of work with feeding, cleaning, and protecting them from predators. But I think you'll find the taste of homegrown meat far superior than what you've purchased in the past.

Speaking of which, the whole point here is to raise animals you plan to eat. In other words, you might want to refrain from naming your dinner. This also means you need to learn how to properly butcher the animals. And this is where many people turn away from the prospect of raising meat animals. Killing and processing a chicken is a whole lot different from heading out to the garden and picking a few tomatoes. If you've never done it before, you're naturally going to feel at least a bit apprehensive. That's normal, it just means you're human. But, that said, it isn't as difficult as you may think and it does get easier the more often you do it.

WILD FISH AND GAME

Hunting, fishing, and trapping have all been putting meat on the dinner table for millennia. While there aren't many of us who could afford to spend hours each and every day pursuing these time-honored activities, they are methods of food production you should consider learning.

First and foremost, research the applicable laws in your area and obtain the proper licenses to engage in these activities. Faithfully observe all rules and regulations that apply. I cannot stress that enough. You may not agree with all of those laws and, in fact, I can almost guarantee there will be at least a few that really bug you. Rather than thumb your nose at them and risk spending hundreds, possibly thousands, of dollars in fines, work to change the laws that don't make sense to you.

Fishing is probably the least energy-intensive of the three methods for procuring wild meat. What could be more relaxing than sitting on shore or in a boat drowning worms all afternoon? Here's the thing, though. The successful fishermen are successful for a reason: They know what the hell they are doing. They know how to "read" the water and accurately predict where they'll find the most fish. They know what bait to use and when to use it (your bait should change based on weather, lighting conditions, and a host of other factors). They've been at it a long time and much of what they do is sort of second nature at this point. The only way you'll ever get to that point is to get out on the water regularly. Talk to the more experienced folks and learn from them. Spend some time hanging around the local bait shop. As long as you're not asking them to divulge their secret spots, most of them will be happy to lend advice.

Where I grew up, deer hunting is treated almost religiously. There are so many kids who go off hunting during deer season, school districts darn near shut down. Of course, the percentage of hunters who bag one or more deer each season is fairly small. But those that do have meat to last for quite some time. There is more to hunting than just going after the big game like deer or moose. Small game will more consistently put meat on the table and the season for it lasts a lot longer than a week or two. A twelve-year-old with a little practice and a used .22 rifle will be able to bring home at least a squirrel or two with almost every outing.

As for trapping, back in the day, many an enterprising young lad made a few extra bucks running a trap line before and after school. That said, this is probably the hardest skill set to learn. There's an awful lot that goes into trapping, from knowing different sets to determining the best locations. There's a fair amount of luck involved as well, truth be told. Out of the entire forest, you need the critter to hit one exact location. By studying the craft you can learn to make your own luck, at least to a degree. Traps are nice in that they work by themselves. While you're doing other things, the traps are (hopefully) bringing in the meat. But there's a lot of work involved in running a successful trap line. The more traps you set, the better your odds of success, of course. You also need to check those traps regularly, preferably daily. The only thing worse than finding an empty trap is finding one that wasn't empty but is now.

As with raising meat, you need to learn how to process wild game and fish. Letting the meat go to waste is just foolish. Practice makes perfect. If you know a hunter, ask them to teach you how to handle this chore.

BEEKEEPING

While man cannot live by honey alone, it can darn sure make things easier to swallow. Honey has been prized for ages and commands a high price, whether sold for cash or bartered. Beekeeping is one of those homesteading types of activities that doesn't involve a lot of daily work. The bees handle most of the heavy lifting. As with anything else, though, there is more to it than it may appear. The hives cost money, whether you buy or build them. Location of the hives is important and can mean the difference between success and failure. Harvesting the honey isn't a walk in the park, either.

All that said, the benefits of producing your own honey are huge. If you have an area that would be suitable for a hive, I'd highly encourage you to explore this option.

FOOD PRESERVATION

All the food in the world won't do you much good if it goes bad before you consume it. Fortunately, there are many ways to safely preserve food, allowing you to learn from mistakes made in the past rather than suffer illness yourself. Two of the more popular methods are dehydration and home canning.

DEHYDRATION

Dehydrating food is simply removing as much moisture from it as possible. There are many different food dehydrators on the market today, with brand names such as Excalibur and Nesco. Most of them work fairly well. Often, the major difference between models and prices is their efficiency. Anything you can dehydrate in one of these commercial gizmos could be dehydrated using your oven as well. That method just takes longer.

There are many plans available online for DIY dehydrators, including those that use solar energy as well as those that utilize lightbulbs. These are definitely worth exploring as building one will be far cheaper than buying one.

HOME CANNING

In the last few years, canning, along with a host of other homesteading skills, have really seen a resurgence in popularity. I see this as being sort of an offshoot to the increase in awareness regarding disaster readiness. Whether that's truly the case or not, the point is that we're seeing something of a renaissance and that's a great thing.

Canning is a skill worth learning and a detailed discussion of it is far beyond the scope of this book. I would highly encourage you to seek out local experts, such as those found through your county extension office, and learn all you can about canning. There is a financial investment here for supplies (pressure canner, jars, lids) but the return on that investment is huge.

It wasn't all that long ago that canning garden produce, as well as meat obtained from hunting, was just a matter of course rather than a mildly interesting hobby. You may even recall your mother or grandmother having jars and jars of soup, stew, chili, beans, and other goodies lining the basement shelves. Canning is an excellent way to preserve your harvest so as to last you through the cold winter months.

SCRATCH COOKING

I know my younger readers may find this difficult to believe, but eating out at restaurants or bringing home takeout used to be a once-in-a-while treat rather than the routine it seems to be today. The vast majority of meals were prepared in the kitchen at home. And few of those meals came out of a box and were simply warmed up on the stove. For darn sure none of them involved the use of a microwave oven. You know what else? Those home-cooked meals were far better than much of anything you'll get in a restaurant today. They looked, smelled, and tasted like real food! Armed with nothing more than flour, salt, pepper, and her cast-iron skillet, my Grannie could fry a chicken that would make Colonel Sanders weep with tears of shame.

Being able to cook entire meals completely from scratch has become something of a lost art. This is due as much to time constraints as anything else, of course. In many households, both parents (assuming they're both present in the home) work and thus don't have the time every day to spend in front of the oven. As a result, more families eat out than ever before. This has led to entire generations missing out on learning how to cook from scratch.

A big part of self-sufficiency is learning these so-called lost arts. Scratch cooking isn't particularly difficult and there are tons of resources available for learning it. The hardest part about it, in fact, might be making the time.

If you are a complete novice, I don't suggest starting out with a full-blown Thanksgiving dinner with all the trimmings. Unless you're really lucky or inherently talented, that's just a recipe for disaster. Instead, start small with something like scratch biscuits or perhaps meatloaf and homemade (not from a box) mashed potatoes. Neither are especially, difficult but they'll get you on the road to developing your skills.

Remember, eating out will probably not be a viable option should there be a collapse. If you can't prepare your food in a safe and tasty manner, it won't matter how big your garden is or how much meat you harvested.

CLEANING PRODUCTS

Making homemade soaps, shampoos, and the like is another self-sufficiency that has seen a surge in popularity recently. Many people have discovered a love of making these as a hobby and, for some, a way to bring in a bit of extra income. Making your own soap allows you to be a bit of a home chemist. While not difficult, it does require precise measuring and the process is rather exacting. Further, in many cases you will be dealing with lye, which is a hazardous chemical and great care must be taken when handling it.

Think about this, though. How much money do you spend each year on soap, shampoo, laundry detergent, and other cleaning products? Probably in the neighborhood of at least a few hundred dollars, perhaps more if you tend to favor the high-end brands. You could easily cut that yearly expense in half by producing your own, plus you'd be in control as to what goes into those products. On top of that, should there be any sort of delay in shipments to the stores, you'd be largely unaffected.

POWER GENERATION

Great strides have been made in recent years in alternative sources of energy. Solar panels, in particular, have dropped in price and dramatically increased in efficiency. While they still aren't rock-bottom cheap, solar panel systems are a worthy investment. They not only allow you to reduce your monthly power bill, but if the grid were disrupted for some reason, you'd likely still be able to power a few appliances.

Portable solar panels are an excellent way to dip your toe into the alternative energy game. Goal Zero produces a range of products, from small, folding panels suitable for keeping your cell phone working to full-blown solar generators. Of course, you could also jump in with both feet and explore a full solar panel system installation for the house. While not a cheap endeavor by any means, there are different government grants and subsidies that can reduce the bite on your wallet. Plus, these systems are truly an investment in that if you decide to sell the home later, such a system is considered a great bonus, unlike most in-ground pools.

Designing and pricing out an entire system is well beyond the scope of this book. However, as a general rule of thumb, your out-of-pocket expenses, taking subsidies into account, will probably be in the thousands. I know one couple who managed to wire most of their home to run on solar for $2,000 or so. But, they did almost all of the work themselves and knew what they needed in terms of panel size, battery backups, and other equipment. If that's not you, then you'll need to call in the professionals. Search online for solar panel suppliers and installers in your area, and see if you can get a few quotes.

Traditional generators, whether fueled by gasoline, natural gas, or propane, are another option. The difference between these and solar panel systems is the traditional generators are more suited for limited use, such as during a crisis, rather than being any sort of long-term power solution. But even a small Honda generator will keep a few things running in a pinch. Again, the overall goal here is to be able to provide for your own needs in an emergency, rather than sit and wait for help to arrive.

SOLAR ELECTRICITY VS. SOLAR WATER HEATING

Take a look at the roof of a home equipped with solar panels. You may notice what seems like two different styles of panels. The slim ones are actually called photovoltaic (PV) panels and the boxy ones are called solar hot water (SHW) panels. PV panels convert solar energy into useable electricity. SHW panels do just as the name would suggest—heat water. The ideal solar panel system would incorporate both types.

HARVESTING WATER

Water, of course, is essential to our lives. We need it for drinking, keeping our animals hydrated, and growing our gardens. In order to become fully self-sufficient, we need to break the tether to municipal water and explore other options.

In former times, wells were dug by hand. Generally, they consisted of a deep hole dug down to the water table. Water would seep in through the sides of the well and fill the bottom. You'd then send down a bucket on a rope to haul up water. Digging a well such as this is a very dangerous undertaking, not one to be entered into lightly.

DRIVING A WELL POINT

If you are in an area where the water table is fairly close to the surface, say within about 50 feet or less, you can drive a well yourself. It isn't a lot of fun and involves a bit of hard work, but it is doable for many people. You'll need a "well point," which is a metal pipe pointed on one end, threaded on the other, and covered in slotted holes. Start by digging a hole about 2 feet deep where you want the well located. An auger works best but a shovel will do. As tightly as can be made by the strength of your hand, screw a metal cap onto the threaded end of the well point. Put the pointed end down into the hole you dug, keep the well point as perpendicular as possible, and begin driving it down into the ground. Keep hammering away until there is only about a foot of the well point above the ground.

Unscrew the metal cap and attach a coupler, which is a small piece of pipe with threads on both ends. Be sure to use plumber's tape or joint compound as this needs to be a watertight seal. Then, attach a length of pipe to the upper end of the coupler, again making a watertight seal. Place the metal cap on the end of that pipe and pound away. Keep repeating this process until you hear a hollow sound when you hit the pipe. This means you've hit water. No, it isn't going to shoot out the top of the pipe like you've hit oil.

When that happens, tie a fishing weight to the end of a long string and slowly feed it down the pipe. You'll know when you've hit bottom because the string will go slack. Pull it back out and measure how much of the string is wet. Keep at it until you reach a point where at least 5 feet of the string comes back wet. Going this deep will help provide the greatest suction for the pump.

Attach a pitcher pump at the top of the pipe, again being sure to have a watertight seal. Follow the manufacturer's guidelines for priming the pump and soon you'll have fresh water on demand. Fair warning: The first few gallons that come out of the ground are going to look pretty nasty. That's perfectly normal and to be expected. Driving down the well point will have sent a lot of dirt down into the water. Once things settle down, you'll be fine.

DRILLING A WELL

For most people, drilling a well is not going to be a weekend DIY project. It requires special equipment and isn't a cheap endeavor. The

SITING A WELL

In most states, the Department of Natural Resources handles all rules and regulations pertaining to wells. As such, they likely have a contact list of companies that can install a well or at least site one properly. It is important to be sure you're in compliance with all of the laws covering the installation and use of wells. Failure to do so could mean you spend thousands of dollars on the project, only to be forced to pour cement into the well to seal it up.

Another option, at least for choosing the location, is to use a dowser or water witch. I know, I know, we're getting into some fairly questionable areas here. But many people have relied upon the services of dowsers for generations, and anecdotal evidence strongly supports they know what they're doing.

cost for drilling depends upon how deep you need to go and through what material. On average, you can expect to pay around $20–$30 per foot. If the ground is particularly troublesome or the well has to be inordinately deep, say a few hundred feet, the price goes up substantially. That's just for the hole, though. You'll then need to add in the costs for the well pump and all the trimmings, which can add up to several thousands of dollars.

Hey, I never said self-sufficiency was cheap or easy. The good news is that once the well is completed and paid off, you won't be paying a monthly water bill ever again.

I would point out, too, that well pumps require electricity to run. If the grid goes down, or you don't have reliable access to electricity, you'll need a different solution. An excellent option is to take a look at what Flojak (www.flojak.com)has to offer. They manufacture a line of hand pumps designed to work right alongside electric well pumps. You can either permanently install them or just keep them on hand for emergency use.

RAINWATER HARVESTING

In addition to wells, harvesting rainwater is an excellent secondary source for water, whether for consumption or for gardens. I highly encourage you to install rain gutters on not only your home but all outbuildings you may have. How much water can you collect with rainwater harvesting? A realistic estimate once you account for things like splashing, evaporation, and such would be about a half-gallon per inch of rain per square foot of your roof. So, 1 inch of rain falling onto a 2,000-square-foot roof comes to about 1,000 gallons of water. The average rain barrel is 55 gallons or so, which means you'd need eighteen barrels to collect just that single inch of rain.

Take a look around your neighborhood. How many homes have rain gutters installed? Of those, how many have visible rain barrels? While these rainwater harvesting systems have become popular, there are still an awful lot of homes lacking them.

If you live in an area where most of the homes are on city water, you may quite possibly be sitting on a gold mine if you have the ability to provide water in a crisis. Most homeowners will be left in the lurch when their faucets run dry, whether as the result of a power outage affecting their well pumps or because the city isn't maintaining the water equipment any longer.

Ideally, you'll have rain barrels at each gutter downspout, preferably multiple barrels daisy-chained together. There are numerous resources online for how to assemble such a system, complete with spigots for easy water access.

I would caution you, though, about using any products designed or marketed for killing bugs in the water as it sits in your barrels. While mosquitoes can be an issue, you're far better off just dealing with them rather than adding any sort of chemicals to the water to kill the larvae. Use window screening over the tops of the barrels instead. The last thing you want to do is complicate the process of turning the rainwater potable.

FILTERING RAINWATER

Water as it falls from the sky is generally pure. Once it has run across your roof, where the birds and the animals play, so to speak, not so much. That's not really an issue if you're just attaching a hose to the rain barrel and watering plants. But if you, your family, or any of your critters will be consuming the water, it should be filtered first. If there is a fair amount of floating debris in the water, pour it through a coffee filter or bandana to remove the bugs and other debris. Once that's done, you may still want to use a commercial filter such as those sold by Berkey, LifeStraw, or Sawyer, just to be safe.

WILD MEDICINALS

Just as with gathering wild edibles, when it comes to medical needs, nature can provide. Many of the drugs we routinely take today for pain, fever, and stomach ailments were originally found in the forests and fields. Guess what? They're still out there today.

Now, I'm not at all saying you should stop visiting your family physician and for darn sure I'm not suggesting you skip the emergency room when stitches are needed. But by learning at least a few local plants that are useful for medical purposes, you'll be ahead of the game should there be an illness or accident during an existing crisis.

You need to learn how to identify beneficial plants and how to properly use them. It is one thing to know that plantain is great for insect bites, but you also need to know that ingesting it isn't going to do squat. Instead, you chew it up a bit, then spit the glop out on your arm or wherever it itches. Yeah, kids tend to love this one. Some plants are used as poultices, others are brewed in a tea.

I would caution you to check at least three different and distinct sources before relying on any sort of natural remedy. All too often, particularly online, writers will essentially copy and paste from one source to another. This tends to spread bad information as often as it spreads facts. Seek out authorities on the subject, those who have the experience with using natural remedies and wild medicinals. Naturally, there is some risk involved with self-diagnosing ailments and treating them with wild medicinals. One of the most difficult aspects of this is dosage. Each individual plant is going to vary with regards to efficacy. But the more you experiment with wild medicinals, the more adept you'll become at gauging the amount of plant to use in each dose.

One excellent resource for learning the basics about wild medicinals is the *Encyclopedia of Herbal Medicine* by Andrew Chevallier (2000, DK Adult). Rosemary Gladstar is another noted authority on the subject.

REPURPOSING

There is a saying from the old days: "Use it up, wear it out. Make do or do without." This is really the core of what we mean by *repurposing*. We Americans tend to generate an awful lot of trash. However, by thinking outside the box a bit, we can often come up with ways to reuse a fair amount of that junk and give it a second life.

For example, cardboard egg cartons can be used to make great homemade fire starters. Simply fill each egg space with dryer lint, then cover with melted crayons. Break them apart after the wax is hard and store them in a shoe box or plastic bag. To use, simply pull apart the cardboard a bit to expose the lint and light with a match or spark.

Empty soup cans can be used in conjunction with trip wires to create makeshift alarm systems. They are also handy for melting wax for fire starters.

Newspaper can be fashioned into small pots for planting seedlings. My wife has been doing that for years, using a little gadget called a PotMaker. We also reuse plastic takeout containers, such as the kind often used for rotisserie chicken, as mini-greenhouses.

The point is this. There's true garbage and then there's trash that could be repurposed. Before tossing away containers and other similar items, consider washing them and reusing them for something else.

Along these same lines, because we live in what tends to be a throwaway society, we often think of things we buy as being disposable. For example, when we find a rip in a shirt or pair of pants, we think nothing of either tossing it into the garbage or perhaps donating it to a thrift store. Next time that happens, consider taking the time to try and patch or sew the rip, allowing you to extend the useful life of the pants. Those skills will be quite handy should the time come when stopping in a department store to buy a replacement pair of jeans just isn't an option.

Learning to become more self-sufficient can be its own reward. Not only will these skill sets help you financially, they tend to impart a great deal of self-confidence. The more you can do on your own, the less you'll need any sort of outside assistance should a collapse of any sort occur.

CHAPTER 9

PUTTING IT ALL TOGETHER: THE HOME OF THE SELF-SUFFICIENT INVESTOR

For some of you, this chapter will be like taking a tour of your home. For most of us, though, what follows is one part dream and one part planning. What we're going to do is put it all together and design an ideal homestead for the self-sufficient investor. It may not be perfect for everyone. In fact, I can guarantee it won't. We all have different circumstances, skill sets, backgrounds, and experiences. We'll at least try and hit most of the high points of what should be considered when setting up *your* ideal self-sufficient homestead.

PROPERTY: THE BIGGEST INVESTMENT OF YOUR LIFE

For most of us, purchasing real estate is likely going to be the single-largest financial transaction of our lives. Obviously, this is not something to enter into lightly. There are many considerations to bear in mind, location being at the top of the list.

Given that most people can't afford to plunk down a ton of cash to purchase a homestead, proximity to work is naturally a big factor. You'll probably need a job to afford the mortgage, right? On top of that, though, take into account your prepper instincts when deciding where to live.

Climate is an important consideration. Being as self-sufficient as possible means being able to produce a large percentage of your food. Human beings for eons have been able to survive through brutal winters on the food and supplies they've stockpiled. But being located in a more temperate climate, one where you can realistically grow food year round, is perhaps a more ideal solution.

If moving to a different part of the country isn't a viable option for you, then you'll need to plan for how for food provisions when the weather turns cold. Greenhouses and hoop houses are certainly doable. Even having small cold frames can extend the growing season by a month or more. Perhaps, if you'll be building or remodeling a home on the property, you can incorporate a large sunroom or greenhouse attached to the main structure.

Past history of natural disasters in the area is another factor. You certainly wouldn't want to locate your homestead on any sort of known flood plain, for example, or in an area known to experience wildfires on a regular basis.

HOW MUCH LAND WOULD YOU REALLY NEED?

Because many factors come into play, this is one question that doesn't have any sort of blanket answer. I've heard of families who can produce enough food to provide for most or all of their needs on as little as a quarter of an acre. Other homesteaders do just fine on a couple of acres or more. The best advice I can give is to purchase as much land as you can reasonably afford. Personally, I feel it is far better to have more land than you need than to come up short.

Another consideration is proximity to other people. On the one hand, you probably won't want to be in a subdivision, let alone in any sort of crowded urban area. On the other hand, though, having at least some people in the general area affords you, at least in theory, some degree of assistance should things take a turn. Plus, few people truly want to live in a bubble with no one else in their lives. Whatever you do, though, avoid homeowner associations at all costs! While there may be some out there that are amenable to homestead activities, I have yet to encounter one of those personally.

Yet another thing to research is the local government that has jurisdiction over your potential homestead location. Do their values mirror your own to a large degree? If not, you're likely best served by looking elsewhere.

When looking at a prospective property, try to imagine all of the future possibilities. Is there space where you could build a workshop or other outbuildings? What about a good-sized pole barn structure, one that you could use to rent space to store boats and such? That could provide a bit of extra income to help offset expenses as you get rolling with homesteading. You'll need areas for gardens, maybe fruit trees, and likely some animals.

Once upon a time, it was believed that real estate was just about as sound of an investment as you could possibly make. It was extremely rare to lose money in the long run on property purchases. A home purchased in 1985 for $75,000 easily doubled in market value within perhaps as little as ten years. The collapse of the housing bubble in the early 2000s changed all that. While property values will likely still increase over time, it won't happen nearly as rapidly as before.

However, bear in mind that the goal here isn't really to invest in real estate but to invest in self-sufficiency. That being the case, we're not quite as concerned about how much the property will appreciate over time as we are about the freedom the property will give us.

There are risks inherent to any investment, whether it be in gold, real estate, or anything else of value. By investing in your own self-sufficiency, though, you are shouldering most of those risks yourself, rather than being beholden to outside factors.

BUILDING THE HOMESTEAD

There are several commonalities among homesteads. These include the house proper, outbuildings, gardens, and natural resources, among others. Let's take them one by one.

HOME

Remember as we go along here that we're talking in generalities. Rather than providing you with some sort of "must have" checklist, these are all merely suggestions, things to get you thinking and planning, taking into account your individual needs.

Forget about any sort of McMansion and think small and energy efficient. Personally, I'm not entirely sold on the "tiny houses" concept that has been popular lately. I just don't know that I'd do well living with my family in a home that has less than 300 square feet or so. That said, the homestead house should be fairly small. The less the square footage, the less energy needed to moderate the indoor temperature, as well as keep clean.

A wood stove will not only provide heat but allow you to cook without being tied to a utility service. Of course, having access to a large propane tank and using that fuel for your stove and other modern conveniences will probably be appreciated by family members. A fireplace looks great, but remember that they are largely inefficient when it comes to actually heating the home, at least when compared to wood stoves.

Relatively few people today, at least here in the United States, are accustomed to using outhouses. An occasional trip to a porta-potty while attending the fair or other event really isn't the same as trekking out the back door at 2 a.m. to use the facility. So, look at either a septic system, which will need to be emptied from time to time, or a composting toilet system.

The home should be built to be as energy efficient as possible. This means all windows should be double-paned and walls should be well-insulated. Plan on using curtains and blinds to keep out the sun on hot days. If you're building from the ground up, take into account the prevailing wind currents and position the home and windows to capture those breezes.

Basements, provided they are allowed where you'll be building, are a great idea. They provide excellent storage space as well as possible living quarters when the heat really cranks up in the summer.

Speaking of storage areas, you'll definitely want a large pantry near the kitchen. At the tail end of the growing season, you'll be canning as much of the garden produce as possible, so you'll need someplace to store it. A root cellar is another great feature, allowing you to keep things like apples and potatoes all winter long.

OUTBUILDINGS

There are a few different outbuildings you may want to consider. The first that comes to mind is a workshop of some sort. On a homestead, you'll be doing most, perhaps all, of your own repairs. A small workbench tucked into the corner of a single car garage might not cut it. My own dream workshop contains several workbenches with a dizzying array of hand tools lining the walls. Rather than a roll-up door like the ones on a traditional garage, mine would have sliding barn doors that would be easier to fix if running to Home Depot wasn't an option. The shop would be large enough that I could pull in a vehicle to service so I don't have to stand on the driveway in the rain or snow.

As we mentioned earlier, having a largish pole barn or similar structure could allow you to rent storage space for boats, cars, and other vehicles or equipment. Of course, this would necessitate other people coming to your homestead to drop off and pick up their vehicles, which may not be ideal, but depending on other factors, you could still maintain some degree of privacy. Also, such a side business would require specific insurance policies, which would cut into your rental income.

If you're planning on having animals of one sort or another, a structure or shelter for them would be ideal. The size and configuration would, of course, depend upon the type(s) and number of animals.

Home brewing wouldn't really require a separate outbuilding, unless you're planning on producing large amounts of alcohol. However, consider combining your activities in one location; in addition to the brewing, for instance, you could boil your maple syrup and perform related activities under one roof.

While not an actual outbuilding, an outdoor kitchen setup is worth considering. If you lack air conditioning, summer months aren't ideal for cooking indoors. Having a covered area adjacent to the house where you can build a wood-fired oven or use a wood stove for cooking and canning is definitely something to think about.

GARDENS

Naturally, a large portion of the self-sufficient diet will come from garden beds. This need not be just one giant garden taking up a large portion of your available space all in one clump, either. Many homesteaders have several garden beds scattered about. Smaller beds can often be easier to maintain as you can easily reach all sides of it when weeding and harvesting. Plus, there's a bit of psychology at work with this approach. Walking out in the morning to a half-acre plot can be daunting when you think about having to weed it all. Looking at a few smaller beds, even if they all add up to the same square footage as the large garden, makes the job a bit easier on the mind if not the back.

AQUAPONICS

Essentially, aquaponics combines growing plants and raising animals into one system. It has become rather popular in recent years, particularly among the self-reliant crowd. The idea is to raise fish in a pool or similar structure, then circulate the water through hydroponic beds, where the nutrients in the water that come from the fish feed the plants. It truly is a neat concept and worth exploring. While tilapia are probably the most common fish raised in this sort of system, you could do other freshwater fish, such as some varieties of perch or catfish, as well as crayfish.

In addition to garden beds, if the climate allows you'll almost certainly want some fruit trees. Given that many varieties require more than a single tree for pollination, plan accordingly.

NATURAL RESOURCES

Readily available water, whether through a drilled well or a stream running through the property, is but one desirable natural resource, though it is indeed an important one.

How much rainfall does the area receive in an average year? Perhaps just as important as the total amounts is *how often it rains*. That sounds silly, I know, but this information is important to know when planning your rain collection system. Your system, no matter how large, will only store a finite amount of water. Knowing it rains infrequently means you'll maybe need a larger system than someone who lives in an area where it rains far more often.

What sorts of flora and fauna call the property home? Take a walk around and look for droppings and tracks to get an idea of the critter population. While hiking about, look for edible or otherwise useful plants native to the region. You *do* know how to recognize them, right? If not, take a guidebook with you, preferably one with color photos.

You'll probably burn wood as your primary source of heat as well as for cooking, so you'll want a fairly large wood lot on the property. Remember, too, that felled trees will need to be cut and split, then the wood seasoned for about a year before it can truly be used for fuel.

POWER GENERATION

The house itself, as well as perhaps a few of the outbuildings, should be built in such a way that the roofs are exposed to strong sunlight throughout the day. This allows you to take full advantage of the solar panel arrays you'll want to install.

Personally, I'm not entirely sold on wind turbines for power generation. I've heard too many stories about them being loud as well as unreliable. Of course, technology is improving every day so this might still be something you'll want to consider when the time comes to build your homestead.

As I said at the outset of this chapter, these are all things you may want present when designing your homestead. My ideal may not be yours, but no matter how large or small, most homesteads have much in common, if not in practice then at least in theory.

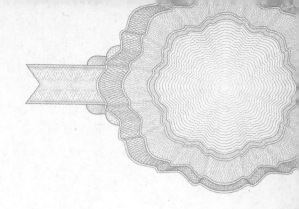

FINAL THOUGHTS

No doubt about it, financial preparedness is a bit different from what we might call "traditional" prepping. Sure, there are commonalities, such as ensuring there is enough food, water, and other necessities for the family in the event of a disaster. But, folks, there is so much more to prepping than buying pallets of freeze-dried food and cases of bottled water.

Financial preparedness, for many people, requires a lifestyle change. It necessitates a conscious decision to go without a few luxuries from time to time and invest in long-term rather than immediate wants. I'm not saying you can't have your double latte. I'm just saying maybe you don't need it every single morning.

It means working hard to get out, and stay out, of debt. Achieving that goal won't be easy, not by any stretch of the imagination. Doing so entails sacrifice and dedication. You may even experience a bit of ridicule from friends, believe it or not. So many people are accustomed to a spend-spend-spend lifestyle, they can't imagine living any other way.

Here's the thing, though. Those who live strictly by credit are in for a rude awakening should even minor bumps in the financial road come to pass. Quite often, in my experience at least, an awful lot of these people live in something like a house of cards. If one of those cards falls, with something like the sudden need for an unexpected car repair, the whole thing is in danger of toppling.

Rather than building a home made from (credit) cards, strive for one built on a solid foundation of financial well-being.

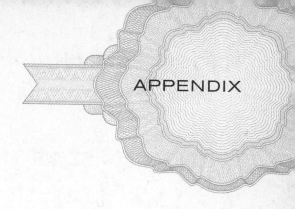

LIST OF BARTER GOODS

As you go through these lists of potential barter goods, keep in mind the three rules we talked about in Chapter 5.

1. The item must have inherent value to you. Don't stock up on stuff that you'd never end up using yourself.

2. The item must be shelf-stable. Avoid any items that will not store well long-term.

3. The item must be relatively inexpensive now. You shouldn't spend a ton of money on these things.

CONSUMABLES

- ❑ Baking staples (flour, sugar, etc.)
- ❑ Beans
- ❑ Garden produce
- ❑ Heirloom seeds
- ❑ Multivitamins
- ❑ Rice
- ❑ Salt
- ❑ Spices, herbs
- ❑ Sweeteners

FOOD PREPARATION

- ❑ Cast-iron cookware
- ❑ DIY rocket stoves
- ❑ DIY solar ovens

FOOD PRODUCTION AND ACQUISITION

- ❑ Air rifle pellets
- ❑ Fishing gear
- ❑ Gardening tools
- ❑ Snare wire
- ❑ Traps

FOOD PRESERVATION

- ❑ Jars, lids
- ❑ DIY dehydrators
- ❑ Pressure canner

WATER FILTRATION AND PURIFICATION

- ❑ Coffee filters or bandanas
- ❑ Commercial water filters (Berkey, Sawyer, LifeStraw, etc.)
- ❑ Water containers
- ❑ Water purification tablets

VICES

- ❑ Alcohol
- ❑ Caffeine tablets
- ❑ Candy
- ❑ Cocoa mix
- ❑ Coffee
- ❑ Tea
- ❑ Tobacco, rolling papers, cheap pipes

MEDICAL SUPPLIES

- ❑ Analgesic ointment
- ❑ Antacids
- ❑ Antibiotic ointment
- ❑ Anti-diarrheals
- ❑ Antihistamines
- ❑ Burn cream
- ❑ Cold remedies
- ❑ Cough syrup
- ❑ Elastic wraps
- ❑ Feminine health products (menstrual pads, yeast infection creams, etc.)
- ❑ Gauze pads
- ❑ Gloves (latex or nitrile)
- ❑ Moleskin dressing
- ❑ Pain relievers, fever reducers (acetaminophen, ibuprofen)
- ❑ Prescription medications

HAND TOOLS

- ❑ Axes
- ❑ Batteries
- ❑ Bungee cords
- ❑ Cordage
- ❑ Generators, solar panels
- ❑ Hammers
- ❑ Hatchets
- ❑ Knives
- ❑ Machetes
- ❑ Paracord
- ❑ Pliers
- ❑ Saws
- ❑ Screwdrivers
- ❑ Sharpening tools
- ❑ Tarps
- ❑ Wrenches

HYGIENE SUPPLIES

- ❑ Baby wipes
- ❑ Dental floss
- ❑ Deodorant
- ❑ Diapers
- ❑ Razors
- ❑ Shampoo
- ❑ Soap
- ❑ Toilet paper
- ❑ Toothbrushes
- ❑ Toothpaste

CLOTHING AND CLOTHING REPAIR

- ❑ Gloves, mittens
- ❑ Knit hats
- ❑ Needles
- ❑ Patches
- ❑ Scarves
- ❑ Shoe Goo
- ❑ Socks
- ❑ Thread
- ❑ Underwear

MISCELLANEOUS

- ❑ Art supplies
- ❑ Baking soda
- ❑ Bleach
- ❑ Board games
- ❑ Books (paperbacks, puzzle books)
- ❑ Candles
- ❑ Canning lids
- ❑ Condoms
- ❑ Dice
- ❑ Fishing supplies (hooks, line)
- ❑ Heavy-duty garbage bags
- ❑ How-to manuals
- ❑ Magnifying glasses
- ❑ Matches, butane lighters, ferro rods
- ❑ Notebooks
- ❑ Pens, pencils
- ❑ Plastic bags (zipper-lock closure)
- ❑ Playing cards
- ❑ Reading glasses
- ❑ Strike anywhere matches
- ❑ Vinegar

INDEX

G

Game, wild, and self-sufficiency, 128–30

Gardening: and barter, 90–91; and homesteading, 149–50; and self-sufficiency, 124–26

Gemstones, 82–85; purchasing, 84–85

Generators: and barter, 94; and self-sufficiency, 135

Germany, and economic collapse, 16–18

Glasses, reading/magnifying, and barter, 98

Global Financial Crisis. *See* Great Recession

Gold, as investment, 70–73; bars, 70–71, 73; chart, 70; coins, 57, 58, 73; jewelry, 71–72; purity, 71, 73; testing, 71–72; weight, 70–71, 73

Great Depression (1929–1940), 19–22

Great Recession (2007–2009), 25–27

Grocery expenses, and debt reduction, 39–41

Gunsmithing skills, and barter, 106–107

H

Hand tools, and barter, 94–95

Handyman skills, and barter, 104

Health expenses, and debt reduction, 42–43

Heirloom seeds, and barter, 91

Herbs, and barter, 92

Hiding valuables: in home, 116–20; outside home, 120–22; poor locations, 116–17

Home brewing skills: and barter, 102–103; and homesteading, 148–49

Home canning skills: and barter, 105; and self-sufficiency, 131–32

Home equity loans, 44

Homeowner associations, 145; and gardens, 127

Homesteading: defined, 124; establishing, 146–51

Honey, and self-sufficiency, 130–31

Houses/homes: and debt reduction, 43–44; and homesteading, 146–48

How-to manuals, and barter, 99

Hunting: and barter, 107; and self-sufficiency, 129

Hygiene supplies, and barter, 95–97

Hyperinflation: defined, 18; in Germany, 17–18

I

Ibuprofen, and barter, 92–93

Income, earning extra, 52–54

Inflation, defined, 17–18

Interest rates: credit card, 35; mortgage, 44

ABOUT THE AUTHOR

Jim Cobb is the owner of Disaster Prep Consultants (www.Disaster PrepConsultants.com) as well as the author of several books, including *Prepper's Home Defense*, *Prepper's Long-Term Survival Guide*, and *Countdown to Preparedness*. Jim also writes for several magazines, such as *Survivor's Edge*, *Self Reliance Illustrated*, *American Survival Guide*, and *OFFGRID*. His primary home online is www. SurvivalWeekly.com, and he can be found on Facebook at www. Facebook.com/JimCobbSurvival. Jim has been involved with disaster planning and mitigation for over thirty years. He lives and works in the upper Midwest with his beautiful wife, their three adolescent weapons of mass destruction, two killer canines, and one cat that greatly exaggerates his importance to life as we know it.